FREEMASONRY
A French View

ROGER DACHEZ
President of the French Masonic Institute

ALAIN BAUER
Freemason

Westphalia Press
An imprint of the Policy Studies Organization

The following works in French have been published by
Presses Universitares de France in the series led by Alain Bauer:

Alain Bauer and Roger Dachez, *Les 100 mots de la franc-maçonnerie*, n° 3799.
Alain Bauer and Roger Dachez, *Les Rites maçonniques anglo-saxons*, n° 3607.
Alain Bauer and Gérard Meyer, *Le Rite français*, n° 3918.
Alain Bauer and Pierre Mollier, *Le Grand Orient de France*, n° 3607.
Roger Dachez, *Histoire de la franc-maçonnerie française*, n° 3668.
Roger Dachez, *Les Rites maçonniques égyptiens*, n° 3931.
Roger Dachez and Jean-Marc Pétillot, *Le Rite Écossais Rectifié*, n° 3885.
Marie-France Picart, *La Grande Loge Féminine de France*, n° 3819.
Andrée Prat, *L'Ordre maçonnique, le droit humain*, n° 3673.
Yves-Max Vinton, *Le Rite Écossais Ancien et Accepté*, n° 3916

FREEMASONRY
A French View

TABLE OF CONTENTS

FOREWORD

French Freemasonry has its own unique perspective, which is not surprising since the world rather expects the French to go their own independent way in most things. And they do! While what we have in this volume is not always at odds with Anglo-Saxon Masonic thinking, it is sufficiently different and fresh in outlook to set us to thinking.

The authors have long and distinguished Masonic careers in the various rites, belong to a baker's dozen of lodges, councils, and conclaves, and are well known for their iconoclastic views. They are part of the leadership that had produced a remarkable flowering of Masonic research in Europe and in particular an extraordinary amount of activity in Paris. Equally notable is that they pursue outstanding public careers as well-known professors as well as leaders in national affairs, quite apart from their busy and sometimes provocative Masonic lives.

When I first encountered both the vast quality and quantity of current French Masonic writing, I wondered if anyone on the other side of the Atlantic was aware of its extent or appreciated the numbers of French scholars who were involved. Quite frankly, although American Masonic membership far exceeds that of France, there is simply no comparison in the depth of research. The annual outpouring of titles and their profundity puts those of us who work in English is a decidedly defensive position.

One reason for this situation that I always cite in a mea culpa is that American Freemasonry provided a social safety net of hospitals, orphanages, retirement homes and other charities which required a much larger membership than in Europe. The emphasis was different, and it would seem peculiar to a French lodge to be sponsoring a juvenile soccer team or raising money for a hospital ambulance. So before apologizing for the relative lack of intellectual activity, one should reflect on the large scale philanthropy that a less elitist approach has supported.

There is no reason though why the efforts of which this book is an example should not be shared by readers in Los Angeles as well as Lyon. After all, a candidate for Masonic degrees is told that one reason he acquires the secrets is in order to travel and work in foreign lands, as the operative masons who built the cathedrals did. The following pages will ably serve those of whatever nationality seeking light.

Paul Rich

St. John's Lodge, Boston

INTRODUCTION

In addition to being a regular marketing subject in the newspapers, Freemasonry is a controversial subject for historians. This is particularly the case in a country such as France, where since the start of the eighteenth century its remarkable story has fostered all kinds of paradoxes. This is one of its main attractions, though also an inexhaustible source of problems and traps for those who study it.

The first of these paradoxes is that in general Freemasons hardly recognize themselves in the portraits drawn up by their observers or enemies (which range from the simply mocking to the resolutely hostile), but remain passionate about anything that gets them talked about. A public institution that has been tightly interlinked with the intellectual, political, social, and religious history of Europe for over three centuries, Freemasonry claims to be the bearer of a subtle truth that by its very nature cannot be understood by what Freemasons see as the "profane" world. This ambivalence is typical of any group that claims that secrecy is a component of its internal identity but that is also unable to ignore the image reflected back to it by its social status—sometimes for the better, and often for the worse. Clearly, this does little to facilitate the work of historians or sociologists studying Freemasonry. Should they ignore the proclaimed primacy of this "profound" identity, which almost certainly escapes outside observers, and therefore limit themselves to a purely phenomenological approach to a much more complex reality, or should they employ participatory ethnology in order to overcome this dilemma? In other words, can we only talk about Freemasonry in a relevant way if we are Freemasons ourselves? But if this is the case, do we not risk merely speaking of it with complacency and without critical spirit? In fact, much of the literature on this issue published over recent decades has permanently wavered between these two pitfalls.

The second paradox, which is certainly no less important than the first, concerns the term *Freemasonry*, the meaning of which is debated even among Freemasons themselves. The vagaries of history and the countless possibilities of human imagination have attributed various paths to Freemasons, in different places and periods. Thus, from a diachronic perspective, Freemasonry has had several lives, several identities, and several faces. On a synchronic level, it juxtaposes and brings into interaction (and even sometimes strong opposition) such contrasting perceptions that it is almost tempting to pluralize Freemasonry, in order to better represent a phenomenon that is difficult to define. From the fantasy image of Freemasonry in the "age of the cathedrals" (if it ever existed in this supposed form), to that of the "little father," Émile Combes[1], engaged in a merciless battle against the Catholic clergy and for the Republic, to that held by Newton's inner circle in England at the end of the seventeenth century (made up of Freemasons interested in alchemy, biblical history, and scientific rationality), or that of the Parisian Enlightenment, where philosophers in Lodges envisaged a different kind of world, Freemasonry encapsulates numerous irreconcilable universes. Moreover, on the geopolitical terrain of contemporary Freemasonry, there are obvious differences between British Freemasonry (a key element of the traditional establishment, with its strong links to the aristocracy and the Church of England, reproducing the "sacred principles of morality" in its rituals) and French Freemasonry. Since the end of the nineteenth century, the latter's familiar image was particularly associated with "social" involvement, and for a

1   Prime Minister of France, from 1902 to 1905.

long time it was very close to the circles of power, in which it sometimes became tangled up, as well as being always a guardian of state secularity and the "absolute freedom of conscience.")

Between a Freemasonry defined as "essentially initiatory," and one that is (in the words of some French Masonic dignitaries) "political by nature," between those who simply wish to receive the Light and those claiming to use it to change society, where is the common ground? What are the fundamental principles linking the two? On what basis can they both claim to be part of Freemasonry? What is the critical distance that separates them?

These are some of the questions that we will attempt to address without preconceptions here. This work is the product of the intersecting reflections of two "participating spectators," who although familiar with the Masonic world and curious about its history, do not seek to impose their own view. Despite their significant differences, they are accepting of one another.

By proposing a dual perspective of both empathy and distance regarding a poorly understood institution, we primarily wanted to give the reader a travel guide to a sometimes confusing world, offering him or her ways of constructing his or her own view with confidence.

PART ONE

HISTORICAL OVERVIEW

CHAPTER I
LEGENDARY AND MYTHICAL ORIGINS

The world of Freemasonry is filled with legends and rituals, and ever since it started attempting to identify its own origins (from the eighteenth century onwards) it has often confused its myths with its history. The way in which its genesis is still sometimes retraced, particularly in France, amply demonstrates this confusion and the touching but damaging amateurism that long dominated Masonic historiography.

However, the account of these mythical origins is useful and instructive. In holding up a mirror to itself in the interests of self-discovery, Masonic thought has projected different images of how it has wanted to be seen, according to the particular place or time. Although the "Authentic School" of Masonic history that was established in England at the end of the nineteenth century[2] and then spread to France much later[3] overcame these pious legends, they nevertheless tell us a lot about the collective unconscious of Freemasonry and allow us to identify the meaning and place of some of the themes seen in its rituals and degrees.

I. THE OPERATIVE MYTH

1. The building of cathedrals: the simplest and most natural hypothesis. Indeed, it is this simplicity that explains the enduring success of this

---

2   Particularly around the Research Lodge *Quatuor Coronati 2076* and its famous annual transactions *Ars Quatuor Coronatorum (AQC)*, a true thesaurus of Anglo-Saxon Masonic erudition.
3   With the masonic review *Renaissance Traditionnelle*, founded by René Guilly-Désaguliers in 1970.

hypothesis. Although modern Freemasons use building tools only as symbols (the mallet, the chisel, the compass, the square, the level, and the plumb line), they are inherited from the "true" or operative (working) masons who worked on building sites in the Middle Ages, as are the symbols that accompany them (the rough stone, the cubic stone, and the tracing board). This theory has been impressively documented by a long and rich historiographical tradition.

There are many archives that testify to the presence of "Lodges" and "Freemasons" on these large building sites from the twelfth and thirteenth centuries onward, in both France and England. The similarities between the material environment and the names used almost imposes the idea of a continuity, or more specifically, of a double continuity.

In a first sense, modern Freemasons can be said to be derived from Freemasons of the past, because towards the end of the fifteenth century, for essentially economic reasons, and above all in the sixteenth century with the Reformation, the golden age of these large and often ecclesiastical buildings came to an end. As constructions became rarer, it is said that Operative Masonic Lodges also suffered the repercussions of this "building crisis," resulting in the idea of using the old method of patronage to survive. By granting honorary membership of the Lodge to an important figure, nobleman, or even a bourgeois, and showing him its mysteries in exchange for a generous donation to the fund for mutual assistance (generally the primary objective of the Lodge and of all brotherhoods at the time), Freemasons attempted to preserve the traditions that they had recorded since at least the fourteenth century through partially legendary tales called the *Old Charges*. This tradition seems to have been strongly established in Scotland, at least in the seventeenth century: a number of local figures were admitted as Gentlemen Masons in various periods. Over time, the decadence of the profession continued. The number of "non operative" newcomers grew as the number of operative members fell. After a few decades, the Lodges contained only non operative members. A new Masonry, later called "Speculative" (*speculatio*: contemplation) Masonry was born, which no longer worked (*operator*: working), but which reflected and meditated, substituting intellectual edifices for cathedrals.

However, there was a form of continuity even more important than this institutional continuity. Because there was a gradual, progressive, and intangible transition with no real break or interruption, the ritual customs and the "secrets of the builders" taught in the Lodges were entirely preserved and passed down to the Speculative Masons. Although they had no professional qualifications and did not use these secrets in practice, the Speculative Masons therefore inherited the operative tradition in its entirety.

It is in this context that the various comments relating to the "art of tracing"—and of course to the famous "Golden Number"—sometimes developed the idea that Operative Lodges, far from being just places of manual work, cultivated superior knowledge on harmonious proportions and "guiding principles," giving a sort of esoteric aura to architecture, and even (with a little imagination) creating links to older philosophical traditions such as those of the Pythagorean School.

Nevertheless, if there was a transition, it did not occur on the continent, where there is no evidence of it. Speculative Freemasonry emerged in Great Britain, and only in Great Britain.

2. The transition in Scotland and England. This is precisely where the difficulties outlined by the Transition Theory of begin to emerge.

This is firstly because for a transition to have occurred the Operative Lodges must still have existed at the end of the fifteenth century or during the sixteenth century: it was only in the seventeenth century that Gentle-men Masons began to be admitted in Scotland. However, everything indicates that in England, where the first Speculative Freemasons emerged in the seventeenth century, these Operative Lodges had disappeared in Tudor times. In Scotland, the Mason Trade underwent major reorganization in 1598 and 1599, under William Schaw (1549 or 1550–1602), Master of Works to the Crown of Scotland and General Warden of Masons, who created from scratch a system of Lodges that was designed not as one of itinerant brotherhoods that were to a greater or lesser extent temporary (the duration of a building project), but as one of lasting and set structures, with a defined geographical attachment. It is here—and here only—that cases of non operative admissions are clearly documented. However, by looking at these cases, we can see that after Gentlemen Masons had been received and paid their contribution, they hardly ever returned to the Lodge that had honored them. In order to transform Operative Lodges into Speculative Lodges, they would have had to participate in their works, and this was not the case. Moreover, these Lodges only met once or twice a year. The situation in England and Scotland therefore almost completely belies the traditional of the Transition Theory.

We need to look again at the meaning of the word *Freemason*. It seems that this word came to designate very different people in the space of a few centuries. In the Middle Ages they were the *freestone masons* (shortened to *freemasons*), a sort of laboring elite who sculpted fine stone, but when the first Speculative Freemasons appeared in England in the seventeenth century, they were literally *free-masons* (or *free and accepted masons*). They were therefore called by the French translation of this name when Masonry began in France: *maçons libres*. But free from what? Undoubtedly from the profession itself, to which they had never actually belonged.

10

We can also observe that since the transition—whatever the truth of it and the means by which it happened—only occurred in Great Britain, the traditional assimilation of Freemasonry and *Compagnonnage* sometimes invoked as a source of the Masonic tradition is unfounded here. Compagnonnage, which appeared in the fifteenth century in France, with customs that we know little about, never gained a foothold in Great Britain in the period that interests us. Moreover, we now know that everything about Compagnonnage that today resembles Masonic customs is in fact the result of extensive borrowing from Freemasonry (rather than the other way around) during the nineteenth century.

3. Towards Speculative Freemasonry: Transition or borrowing?
It is fairly clear that an apparently simple theory that was unanimously accepted for decades is actually almost indefensible. Consequently, we have progressively gone from the transition model to that of borrowing in order to account for the emergence of Speculative Masonry.

"Borrowing" here refers to Speculative Freemasonry in seventeenth-century England, feeling its way and through undoubtedly nonconcerted initiatives, being progressively created by men who called themselves "free-masons." In many cases we do not know how they came to be called this, although the Scottish model may provide a clue: once Gentlemen Masons had been admitted to a Lodge, they took this name and in turn transmitted it, under their own conditions and for their own reasons, which had nothing to do with the masonry profession. They could do this because they were "free."

The political and religious situation at the time, which was unstable and sometimes bloody, explains the abundance of discreet and even secret circles of all kinds in England from the mid-sixteenth to the end of the seventeenth century. Very early on, it seems that Masonry brought together people who shared certain intellectual interests and who prioritized the wish to live side by side with other men and associate with them outside of the (literally) mortal conflicts of politics and religion. The use of conventional signs, symbols, and code language was frequent at the time. Those provided by the ancient traditions of the brotherhood of Masons could serve this purpose. Moreover, Masonry could easily offer noble architecture and abundant philosophical developments, as already shown by copious literature since the end of the Renaissance.

This early Speculative Freemasonry could be found in London in around 1717; all Freemasonry around the world would stem from it.

II. THE TEMPLAR MYTH

1. From the condemnation of the Templar to the literary revival of chivalry. With supposedly Templar sources, an independent myth became linked with Masonic history. Nevertheless, it should be emphasized that the alleged role of the Templars in the creation of Freemasonry was only evoked quite late on—around the middle of the eighteenth century in France, and not until the start of the following century in Great Britain—when the structures and customs of Masonry had already been established for a long time. In fact, outside of the romantic fantasies that are rife among certain contemporary authors, the Templar myth was at first independently constructed to cater for various public interests. A reminder of the main stages of this is useful here.

The posthumous fate of the Templars (who actually had little esteem during the heyday of their order) was undoubtedly linked to the iniquitous conditions of their condemnation and to the poor reputation of the main figures behind it, namely Philip IV of France and Pope Clement V. Various authors publicly supported the theory of the innocence of the "Martyr Order" from the sixteenth century onwards. During the same period (that of the Hermetic-Kabbalistic Renaissance), and based on the confessions of certain Templars when tortured, the idea spread that the Order of the Temple had hidden secret knowledge and used mysterious initiations. Towards the end of the seventeenth century there was a resurgence of interest in the history of knightly orders, and several successful works made the public familiar with the splendor and legends of the ancient knights. One example is the very famous *Histoire de la condamnation des Templiers* by Pierre Dupuy, published in 1654 with four new editions until 1751.

At the turn of the eighteenth century, when the chivalry of old (one might almost say "operative chivalry") was nothing more than a distant memory, the chivalric ideal, which was far removed from the austerity of the end of Louis XIV's reign and the follies and excesses of the *Régence*, experienced a revival. This was a phenomenon of social history: when organized Speculative Freemasonry appeared, at the start of the eighteenth century, chivalry was already a fashionable theme.

2. The world of chivalry and Templar Masonry in the eighteenth century. Although the theme of chivalry eventually became integrated into Masonic heritage, from the end of the 1730s the Templars were initially absent. Thus, in the famous *Discourse* by Ramsay (1686–1743), "Orator for the Grand Lodge" in Paris in 1736, a text which went down in history in France and throughout Europe, the presumed founders of Freemasonry during the Crusades were the Knights of Saint John of Jerusalem: the Knights of Malta, who were the traditional enemies of the Templars. Nevertheless, in a Masonic environment that at the time was heavily influenced by the aristocracy (particularly in France and in Germany, where Masonry would soon spread), the comparison with chivalric knightly orders was quick to convince. Soon, in a second stage, the most prestigious order emerged: the Order of the Templar, which lent itself to such recuperation, precisely because it had ceased to exist at least four centuries before.

The first chivalric-themed Masonic degree, the Knight of the Orient and of the Sword, which was the supreme degree of continental Freemasonry from 1740 to 1750, was not related to the Templars. In it, knights work to reconstruct the Temple of Jerusalem, holding their sword in one hand and their trowel in the other: a clear reminder of an episode in the Bible. However, from 1750, there was a Sublime Knight Elect degree, a forebear of the famous Knight Kadosh, which spread in France ten years later. In the same period in Germany, a Masonic system of Strict Templar Observance was emerging. It would be highly popular for around twenty years. Taking the Templar myth to its full extent, the Strict Templar Observance told that Freemasonry, under the peaceable face of a brotherhood of builders, was actually the Order of the Temple (hidden since its dissolution), and that the "Poor Fellow-Soldiers of Christ and of the Temple of Solomon" had found refuge among the brotherhoods of builders in Scotland. This brought things full circle, connecting the Templar myth to a more traditional history of Freemasonry.

However, just as any theory of a secret survival of the Order of the Temple is nothing but fantasy (as experts on the issue all agree), any idea of a Templar origin behind Freemasonry, however distant and indirect, is unfounded. The persistence of the Templar idea in Freemasonry tells us much about a significant change in the Masonic consciousness that occurred around the end of the eighteenth century. Moving further and further from operative and working references (which were likely judged to be not particularly positive), the original brotherhood deliberately moved closer to the fantasy model of a military and religious order, with its hierarchies, its rules, and its pomp. Although the first Freemasons, who were mostly aristocrats, especially in France, were more comfortable with this, their successors (soon to be mostly public and bourgeois figures) drew from it a sort of substitute nobility, which often flattered their pride, if not their vanity.

However, despite the brilliant and lasting success of Masonic chivalry (Templar or otherwise), it has provoked harsh criticism throughout its history. One example can be seen in the uncompromising words of Joseph de Maistre (1753–1821), who before the French Revolution was himself a Freemason, and a member of a Templar-inspired Masonic system: "What is a knight, when he is created in an apartment in the candlelight, and his honor evaporates as soon as the door is opened?"

III. THE ALCHEMICAL AND ROSICRUCIAN MYTH

1. Rosicrucians and Illuminati: from legend to history. Within Templar legend, there are complementary or alternative fables. Alchemists and the Rosicrucians have often been cited as the hidden founders of Freemasonry. This is supposedly proven by the presence of obvious alchemical symbols in Masonic decorations and traditions, such as the salt and the mercury in the reflection room where the candidate must wait before the initiation, as well as in the "trials" of water, air, or fire during the initiation ceremony. The masonic degree of Rose-Croix, famous in France since the start of the 1760s, seems by its very name to defy any argument or comment. It was not long before a new tale was built on the basis of these uncertain links. Once again, the presumed involvement of these hidden actors in history was only evoked quite late in the eighteenth century, so it is by no means a cornerstone of Freemasonry.

The same applies to the Illuminati, who have been brought back into fashion, or at least into the public eye, by the global success of *The Da Vinci Code*. Although one might appreciate the popular novelist's imagination, historians can only lament the confusions caused by a dubious presentation of the facts, which leads readers to believe that the tale recounts truths that history has forgotten. Yet there is no line of descent (even merely a claimed one) linking men like Galileo and Copernicus, who on the cusp of the Renaissance attempted to shake off the intellectual yoke of almost twenty centuries of fossilized Aristotelianism in order to explore the laws of nature (braving the fury of the all-powerful Church), to the political activists in Germany who, at the end of the eighteenth century under the name "Illuminati" and in the form of a short-lived secret society, dreamed of overthrowing "the throne and the altar" everywhere in Europe. It is pure fantasy to club them all together under the same name and present them as a brotherhood which has existed continuously from the sixteenth century to the present day. It is therefore entirely illogical to present them as the precursors of Freemasonry.

Neither the true Rosicrucians (whom we will discuss shortly) nor the Illuminati (some of whom actually were also Masons)—and less still Leonardo da Vinci or any of his contemporaries—ever played the slightest role in the birth of Freemasonry. In fact, Freemasonry only emerged a century after the Rosicrucians, and existed long before the Illuminati; it violently rejected them, and continued to prosper after they themselves were gone.

However, as is the case with many legends, these exaggerated tales borrow from and distort real historical phenomena.

2. The intellectual sources of Speculative Freemasonry. Speculative Freemasonry does not take its decorations, its symbols, and its principles from the old masonic profession alone. It drew upon the very specific intellectual and cultural context of seventeenth-century England, which, a century after France, had just received and was beginning to incorporate Renaissance thought.

It is necessary to mention the Hermetic-Kabbalistic current among the sources that influenced Freemasonry, which drew upon and borrowed from it. Frances Yates[4] of the Warburg Institute in Great Britain spent

---

4   See in particular: Frances Yates, *The Occult Philosophy in the Elizabethan* Age (London: Routledge, 1979); Yates, *The Rosicrucian Enlightenment* (London: Routledge, 1972).

around forty years studying this subject in depth, along with François Secret,[5] Antoine Faivre,[6] and Jean-Pierre Brach[7] in France at the Paris École pratique des hautes études. Through the rediscovery of the *Corpus hermeticum*, translated in 1463 by Marsile Ficin (1433–1499) in Florence, and after the founding works of Pico della Mirandola (1463–1494) (*Conclusiones philosophicae, cabalasticae et theologicae*, 1486) or Johannes Reuchlin (1455–1522) (*De verbo mirifico*, 1494; and *De arte cabalistica*, 1517), and the fatal brilliance of Giordano Bruno,[8] Europe was fascinated for at least two centuries by *prisca theologia*, *philosophia perennis*: wisdom thought to have come from the depths of time, sculpting and even heralding Christianity (or so it was thought) by integrating it into a sort of universal revelation. The Kabbalah, which was borrowed from the Jews to become the "Christian Kabbalah," also showed, by "the play of numbers and letters," how sacred texts could yield new fruits for those who deciphered them. All the abundant alchemical literature of the same period drew upon this climate of intellectual enthusiasm and linked the ancient art of fire, the physical object of which was chimerical, to the light of this new and yet also most ancient knowledge, to create a spiritual path expressed allegorically in laboratory work: a sort of "speculative alchemy."

It was precisely out of these speculations that a whole world of enigmatic, allusive, and little-explained images, figures, and symbols would emerge. It was particularly abundant in a literature that was extremely widespread and very popular from the late fifteenth to at least the late seventeenth century: that of the *Emblemata*. These were works filled with vignettes, each of which bore a picture with a saying, word, or rather obscure

---

5   François Secret, *Les Kabbalistes chrétiens de la Renaissance* (Paris: Arma Artis, 1985).

6   Antoine Faivre, *L'Ésotérisme (Paris: Puf, 1982).*

7   Jean-Pierre Brach, *La Symbolique des nombres* (Paris: Puf, 1994).

8   Frances Yates, *Giordano Bruno and the Hermetic Tradition* (Chicago: University of Chicago Press, 1964).

short comment, leaving the reader to find the hidden meaning and let their creative imagination run wild. In these countless and curious books there were, from the sixteenth century and—it goes without saying—outside of any Masonic context, many representations of the square, the compass, and the cubic stone, which were associated with various virtues. Masonic emblems therefore existed long before organized Freemasonry.

In the early seventeenth century (from 1614 to 1616), the Rosicrucians published three anonymous manifestos: the *Fama fraternitatis*, the *Confessio fraternitatis*, and the highly strange and fascinating *Chymical Wedding of Christian Rosenkreutz*. The first tells of the legend of the founding father, "C.R.C.," who learned all the knowledge of the Orient on his travels. This was buried by his disciples after his return and supposed death in Europe in 1484. His body was miraculously discovered intact by their successors, 120 years later, in a crypt filled with symbols. Out of this, a secret brotherhood was born, which travelled all of Europe to prepare for the dawn of a new "Christian Republic." In the *Chymical Wedding*, Rosenkreutz makes an initiatory journey into a fabulous palace, where the alchemical process occurs in a sort of sacred drama. Today, we know that there was never a Rosicrucian Order in the fifteenth, the sixteenth, or even the seventeenth century when the manifestos appeared. The word *ludibrium*, meaning "practical joke" or "hoax," was used by one protagonist of this affair, Johan Valentin Andreae (1586–1654), a member of the "Circle of Tübingen," a group of Lutheran theology students which met in the early 1600s. These young idealists dreamed of a more tolerant, more peaceful world reconciling faith and emerging science, and had expressed this hope in the form of an allegorical tale: a game, in a way, but a "serious game." Many distinguished thinkers all around Europe fell for it and, being unable to join the inaccessible Rosicrucians (for a good reason!), in turn embellished this theme. Their writings use the Kabbalistic doctrines, moral emblems, and alchemical symbols: the language of a whole environment and a whole age. Later, without realizing it, early Freemasonry would draw upon this.

However, there was no "conspiracy of the wise," no secret plan from which Freemasonry was born. Although some of the first known Freemasons in England, such as Elias Ashmole or Robert Moray, have been described as Rosicrucians, this was through mistake or confusion. They were interested in the Hermetic-Kabbalistic current echoed in the Rosicrucian manifestos, but they did not belong to a mysterious brotherhood of this name (because it did not exist as such), and they were not the bearers of a mission. They were "received" into Freemasonry, but they did not create it. This does not mean that they did not influence it; but that is another matter.

Ultimately it is the political, religious, and intellectual situation in Great Britain at the end of the seventeenth century, at the time of what the historian of ideas Paul Hazard so aptly called the "crisis of European consciousness," that can provide the keys that will allow us to understand the emergence of Freemasonry.

CHAPTER II
BIRTH IN BRITAIN

I. THE FOUNDATION IN JUNE 1717

When, on June 24, 1717, four Lodges and "some old Brothers" met on the first floor of the little Goose and Gridiron tavern in the Saint Paul's area of London to start the first Grand Lodge, Speculative Freemasonry already had several decades of history behind it. In the second half of the seventeenth century "free" masons in England and Scotland had sometimes held "lodges." These were small, generally short-lived gatherings, and we do not know exactly what kind of work took place there. The foundation in the summer of 1717 in London did not in itself have many consequences, and the only decision was to meet again a year later.

At this time, Freemasonry in London essentially consisted of small artisans, shop owners, modest bourgeois, and a few soldiers. Its main aim was mutual assistance and aid. However, this creation took place in a special context. After the ascension of the Hanovers in 1714 with King George I, there was a final push from supporters of the Stuarts (the dynasty ousted from the throne), leading to the 1715 Rebellion. The defeated "Jacobites" (the royalists who continued to support King James II after he was dethroned by the Glorious Revolution in 1688) had to admit that they really had lost. From 1716, civil peace returned. There was hope for the future, if the English people could be reconciled among themselves under a new king. Perhaps unknowingly, Freemasonry was one of the parts of this strategy.

Although the first Grand Master, Antony Sayer, was just a modest bookseller, his successor in 1718, George Payne, was Secretary to the Tax Office. However, in 1719, something surprising happened: the new Grand Master was Jean-Théophile Desaguliers (1683–1744), a Church of England minister and Curator of the Royal Society. He worked closely with Newton, the then most respected thinker in Europe. He was of French descent and belonged to a family of Huguenots that was exiled when the Edict of Nantes was revoked in 1685. He had become a renowned scientific speaker and would be Chaplain to the Prince of Wales. Above all, he was close to the new authorities, and in 1721 had the Duke of Montagu (himself very representative of the Hanover aristocracy and the richest man in England) elected Grand Master. At the start of his mandate, he made a large donation to the Grand Lodge's common box.

This gave an unambiguous political message, which changed the future of English Freemasonry. It soon attracted all the intellectual and noble aristocracy, who took control, created new and formerly unknown Masonic dignities, organized the work of Lodges to make it more solemn, and padded out the rituals. Gradually, numbers grew to unexpected levels: there were around fifty Lodges in 1723, and almost three times more a decade on, throughout the whole country. A real social and intellectual transformation had occurred: Freemasonry was to become an important institution of the British establishment.

In 1723, with the help of a Scottish pastor, James Anderson (1679–1739) (who used the opportunity to draw abundantly on the archives of his father's Lodge of Aberdeen), the Grand Lodge compiled all the *Old Charges* to write the *Constitutions*. This fundamental work is to this day almost uniquely considered as the founding charter for Freemasonry worldwide.

Indeed, all that remained was for Freemasonry to conquer the world. The conquest began in France.

II. ARRIVAL IN FRANCE

For a long time, Lodges usually met in inns. It was in one such inn, the *Au Louis d'argent*, on rue des Boucheries, in the Saint-Germain quarter of Paris, that France's first Lodge was created in 1725. There were therefore Freemasons in France, but they were not French: only exiled Britons.

From the Glorious Revolution in 1688, there was a massive Jacobite exodus to France, bringing in several thousand people (forty thousand, according to certain sources), particularly to the Saint-Germain-en-Laye region, an area of royal residence. According to Masonic tradition, from this time, there were two Lodges functioning around two Irish regiments: the Dillon Regiment and the Walsh Regiment. Although it is not proven that Freemasons were present in military ranks at this time, it is not absolutely impossible, given that regiment Masonry would later become very widespread. Nevertheless, these two hypothetical Lodges left no documentary evidence. In these circumstances, we might assert that the Paris Lodge was the first official Lodge.

It was led by one of the Jacobite party leaders, Charles Radcliffe, Count of Derwentwater (born in 1693). He was hung in London in 1746, a martyr to the Stuart cause. In the 1720s, he gathered Masons from Scotland and Ireland around him. At first, they worked discreetly in the capital. Derwentwater, sure that they would return to England once victory was secured, gave them only one piece of advice: not to let the French in. His advice was not heeded. In 1737, Paris already had half a dozen Lodges with French members. In 1744, there were more than twenty, and at least as many in the rest of the country. This trend continued throughout the century.

From 1728, the Duke of Wharton (1698–1731), a fanciful and debauched aristocrat who had been Grand Master in London in 1722, having gone over to the side of the Stuarts, had to flee England for France. As shown by a document from 1735, signed by Hector <u>Macleane</u> (one of Derwentwater's first comrades in arms), Freemasons in France recognized the duke as their first Grand Master. There was not yet a Grand Lodge in France, and one was not created until very late on, but there was at least a Masonry that (again, for more political than really Masonic reasons) considered itself independent from London.

The first French Grand Master did not appear until 1738. Unsurprisingly, he was a high-ranking aristocrat: Louis-Antoine de Pardaillan de Gondrin (1665–1736), Duke of Antin and an old playmate of Louis XV. Freed from its English roots, the Masonic Order in France had an auspicious beginning, as we will see.

III. THE FIRST MASONIC DISPUTES

In England, after around 1740, Freemasonry turned its back on the intellectual aspirations perhaps shown by Desaguliers's traveling companions. Having stabilized around the middle class (the gentry kept the high dignities of the Grand Lodge for itself, and the role of Grand Master soon went to the royal family), to this very day it has set a Masonic model of fraternal sociability and shown a marked interest for good works. All of this was based on social and religious conformity, with all political discussion banned (although the tone remained very conservative), which gave rise to the primordial role, never lost, that English Freemasons gave to Lodge rituals and ceremonies. From 1725, Ireland, then Scotland in 1736, followed in England's footsteps. They created their own Grand Lodges, but for reasons of national pride, still claimed original characteristics. Although real, these did not go against the general direction of the English model.

Consequently, it was from Masonic rites that the first disagreements between Freemasons arose: there would be many others, both on the continent and in Great Britain. The most famous was the one that caused around sixty years of conflict between the Grand Lodge, created in London in 1717, and another Lodge, set up between 1751 and 1753. The latter, whose members were mostly Irish (often scorned by the English), developed a Masonic system that differed from that of the first Grand Lodge in several ways, including the arrangement of Lodge officers, the ceremonial processes, and the use of certain symbols. Its members derisively described the practices of the 1717 Grand Lodge as "Modern", criticizing it for deliberately changing old customs. The "new" Grand Lodge, in contrast (and undoubtedly in provocation), took the name "Antient Grand Lodge", which in the eyes of its founders gave it greater authenticity.

Today, it is difficult to separate truth from propaganda in all these accusations. In a few years, the two Grand Lodges were borrowing from each other. Brothers regularly moved between them, and it is difficult to identify the slightest difference between the mindsets of members. Helped by the parochial attitude, scandal was rife between them: a scathing attack, entitled *Ahiman Rezon* ("Help to a Brother" in approximate Hebrew), written in 1751 by the leader of the Ancients, Laurence Dermott, and published in 1756, harshly criticized the Moderns. This continued until 1813, when the two Grand Masters were the King's two sons, and the decision was taken to unite the two Grand Lodges. The union was achieved without much difficulty, creating the United Grand Lodge of England, which was officially set up on December 27, 1813, and still considers itself the "Mother Grand Lodge of all the Grand Lodges in the world."

CHAPTER III
EXPANSION IN THE ENLIGHTENMENT

I. FRANCE: "MASONRY'S ELDER DAUGHTER"

Around 1725 in Paris, a few Jacobite political immigrants from England, Scotland, and Ireland created the country's first Masonic Lodge on rue des Boucheries, in the quartier Saint-Germain. For several years, it remained quiet, and the small circle of France's first Freemasons initially included no French citizens.

However, from 1736, everything changed. Freemasonry, and the "frimassons," as they were called at the time, became fashionable and attracted public curiosity. Before long, the quiet conventicles of British subjects aroused police suspicion. There were searches, and some members of the second order were detained for several days. However, these incidents were minor. In a few years, the movement would not only spread throughout the whole country, it would also become truly French: there were a dozen Lodges in 1737, and forty or so in around 1744, over twenty of which were in Paris. There were perhaps around a thousand Freemasons in France at this time, and numbers would grow to around fifty thousand before the Revolution. In 1738, as mentioned above, the first French Grand Master was the Duke of Antin. For around thirty years from 1743, the position was occupied by Louis-Antoine de Bourbon-Condé (1772–1804), Count of Clermont and a *prince du sang*. At a time when freedom of assembly did not yet exist, the Freemasons were thus safe from serious harassment. Until the end of the nineteenth century, their legal status remained the same: they were "tolerated by the government."

In the anglophilic atmosphere of the Triple Alliance,[9] and despite the resurgence of hostilities during the Seven Years' War (1757–1763), the craze for clubs helped Masonry to grow. When the young Voltaire, in his *Lettres philosophiques*, or *Letters Concerning the English Nation* (1734), celebrated the merits of British society, the cream of French society gathered in the Lodges to share with good bourgeois citizens, in a ritual environment that was both exotic and solemn, a new form of sociability based on "mysteries" (albeit modest ones). During the never-ending festivities, everyone got a taste of the key element in Lodges' work at the time: what they called the "charms of equality."

Born in Great Britain, it was from France that Masonry would conquer Europe, where many Lodges called themselves "daughters of Clermont" throughout the eighteenth century.

II. THE ARISTOCRACY OF THE "HIGH" DEGREES

The democratic form and the apparent equality that constituted the law of the Lodges, imitating English ways, should not be taken at face value: transplanted onto French soil, the rules of Freemasonry evolved, and many Masters of Lodges (particularly in Paris) kept their positions for life, without annual reelection. The provincial Lodges only applied the general principle of election from 1773. The Masonic protocol never really abolished social distinctions; it was reported at the time of the Count of Clermont's accession to the head of the "regular Lodges of the Kingdom," that he would "remove anyone who was not a gentleman or a good bourgeois man."

This interference of social considerations was undoubtedly related to the vogue for high degrees, which appeared from the start of the 1740s. Although

---

9   Alliance signed in The Hague on January 4, 1717, between the Estates General of the United Provinces, King George I of Great Britain, and the Regent Philippe of Orléans, on the initiative of Cardinal Dubois, senior minister in France.

not all originated in France, the country adopted them with great enthusiasm. Throughout the whole of the eighteenth century, the "blue degrees" (the first three) were usually quickly bestowed, with the first two generally given on the same evening. They served as a propaedeutic wave and a simple introduction, but the "Masonic career" for an average Freemason in the Enlightenment above all meant passionately pursuing and receiving these new degrees, the creation of which progressed solidly until the end of the 1770s. Constantly renewing the "pleasures of Masonry," they were the subject of all Masonic concerns and the main center of interest for Freemasons at the time. This world of the "high" degrees also led to the emergence of new hierarchies and new dignities, allowing for a sort of selection among Masons. It "ennobled" certain Brothers of bourgeois origin, for whom the degrees were a form of symbolic reward. The English were more pragmatic and saw them as "side degrees," which were not necessarily superior to the others.

III. THE QUESTION OF FRENCH MASONIC UNITY

Most of the disputes that soon arose, which had a profound effect on Masonic life in France in the eighteenth century and over the following years, came about because of these new degrees. At a time when the central political powers still had few ways of combating local feudalisms, the Grand Lodge (the name of which appeared towards the end of the 1730s, but which had no tangible administrative significance until the 1750s), placed under the nominal but distant authority of the Grand Master, really struggled to combat self-proclaimed provincial structures, such as the "Grande Loge des Maîtres réguliers de Lyon" (Lyon Grand Lodge of Regular Masters), which from 1760 to 1766 held out against what it called the "Grand Lodge of Paris, supposedly of France."

The transformation, from 1771 to 1773, of the first Grand Lodge into the National Grand Lodge of France, later known as the Grand Orient de

France, came at the cost of a split: a Grand Lodge, or Grand Orient "of Clermont," continued to exist, but struggled to survive, until it rejoined the "mother house" in 1799. However, barely half a dozen years later, as England was preparing to definitively resolve the issue by creating a United Grand Lodge of England (which survived until 1813), a new rupture led to the reappearance of two institutional sectors on the French Masonic scene.

To this day, the problem of French Masonic unity, marked by a form of compulsive fission, has not been resolved.

IV. ILLUMINISM AND FREEMASONRY

The new degrees, which spread widely thanks to the success of Freemasonry throughout the country, had a second impact on the Masonic world. They introduced numerous esoteric themes, which were initially almost absent from the top three degrees: alchemy, Hermeticism, the Kabbala, and references to seventeenth-century Rosicrucianism. From moralizing and "humanist" content, Masonry imperceptibly moved to a more spiritual, or even mystical, register.

The most characteristic illustration of this is what is generally called "Masonic Illuminism." It was embodied in several Masonic systems, such as the Rectified Scottish Rite, created in the late 1750s and based on "Templar" Masonry in Germany. It developed in France between 1768 and 1782, around Lyon, thanks to the teachings of a magician of uncertain origin, Martinez de Pasqually (1727[?]–1774), founder of the "Ordre de Chevaliers Maçons Élus Coëns de l'Univers", which had theurgical ambitions. During the 1780s, the flamboyant Cagliostro made a similar proposal for an "Egyptian" Masonry, which was essentially magical. Other possible examples are the Illuminés d'Avignon, who at the same time, led by Joseph-Antoine Pernéty (who in 1758 authored a Hermetic and mythical dictionary: *Dictionnaire mytho-hermétique*), consulted a mysterious oracle in the

Lodge. Joseph de Maistre, who had been familiar with these circles before the Revolution, described those who (without distinction or unfavorable connotations) he called the *Illuminés* (Illuminati) in the following way:

> I am not saying that all Illuminati are Freemasons. I am simply saying that all those I have encountered, particularly in France, are. Their fundamental dogma is that Christianity as we know it today is nothing more than a *Blue Lodge* made for vulgarity, but that it is for *he who desires* to move up through the degrees until he attains sublime knowledge, such as was held by the first truly enlightened Christians. This is what some Germans have called *transcendental Christianity*. This doctrine is a mixture of Platonism, Origenianism, and Hermetic philosophy, on a Christian foundation.

> The main goal of their works and hopes is supernatural knowledge. They have no doubts that man can communicate with the spiritual world, talk to spirits, and thus discover the rarest mysteries.

Although the fate of French Masonry in the nineteenth century gave it much more rationalist and societal commitments, this more or less underlying Illuminist current remained present in France, gaining strength again in the mid-twentieth century and once again becoming one of the familiar aspects of the country's Masonic life.

V. MASONIC COSMOPOLITANISM AND THE AMERICAN TREND

Drawing up a simple portrait of Masonic thought in Enlightenment France is not something that should be attempted. On the one hand, it integrated the old intellectual foundations of the Masonic institution (those which it had inherited from the Renaissance), as well as speculations from its partial Illuminist conversion. On the other hand, the cosmopolitan spirit emerging from Ramsay's *Discourse* was echoed in all the Lodges, and the idea that "the stranger is my Brother" was a sort of universal credo of Masonry in the whole of Europe, and particularly in France. Undergoing cultural, religious, and soon major political change, the continent was preparing for multiple revolutions, and the concerns of Lodges were related to this. Strangely, the winds of history were seen in America first, and the involvement of Freemasonry is undeniable.

It has become a commonplace to say that the American Revolution, centered on the War of Independence, was a Masonic revolution. This statement contains elements of both exaggeration and truth. Since the 1730s, Freemasonry had spread massively in the American colonies, and it was quite deeply rooted in the social fabric. The Ancient Grand Lodge, whose members were more from the lower classes, had shown more progress than that of the Moderns, which was directly connected to the London powers. The founding incident of the revolt, the famous Boston Tea Party, was an initiative planned through a Boston Lodge, in its meeting place, the Green Dragon Tavern. Many of the revolutionary leaders were Masons, with George Washington himself obviously at the forefront. The Founding Fathers were mostly Founding Brothers.

From La Fayette to Rochambeau, there were many Freemasons among the young liberal nobles of the mid-1770s who were attracted to the cause of the American "Insurgents," and they played a major role in convincing Louis XVI to help the Americans shake off the English yoke. Once it had won its independence, America built a new political world, giving Freemasonry a key place in its social and institutional imagination. It is often said that the town of Washington bears the mark of this, although some associations are clearly incorrect or illusory. However, the famous painting showing Washington in Masonic decorations, laying the cornerstone of the Capitol building, surrounded by Brothers from his Lodge, following a ceremonious parade in the town (an unthinkable sight in France), is not a myth. It remains an eloquent testimony of Masonry's involvement in the founding events of the United States.

VI. ENLIGHTENMENT MASONS AND THE FRENCH REVOLUTION

*M*utatis mutandis, it is also interesting to look at Freemasonry's role in another, even more emblematic revolution: the French Revolution. From the end of the eighteenth century, this question has caused constant historiographical disagreements. Today, it is possible to offer a more reasonable, contrasting, and balanced assessment.

Undeniably, the ideas of equality, tolerance, and universal fraternity, which had been so vital in the Lodges for several decades, fitted easily with the currents of thought leading to the Revolution. It is also clear that some important leaders of the movement were known Freemasons: La Fayette (with all his contradictions) is a typical example, but there were many others. From here, it is just a small step to conclude that Freemasonry prepared, and even steered, the French Revolution. The school of history closely linked to the Far Right in France was quick to make this leap: this is the traditional "conspiracy theory," started by the Abbé Barruel at the end of the eighteenth century, and notably supported by French historians such as Gustave Bord and Bernard Faÿ in the twentieth – both of them being hostile to Freemasonry. Strangely, it was taken up at the end of the nineteenth century by "progressive" Freemasons who were proud to claim such descent. Yet the facts do not support such a simplistic theory.

We know that the supposed egalitarianism of the Lodges never eliminated social distinctions; the Brethren always separated "game" and reality. Although many Freemasons were at the forefront of the Revolution, this was partly because the first to benefit from the movement, the bourgeoisie, had long been the main recruits of Freemasonry: this created a clear statistical bias.

It was also because the king, when he called the Estates General (the aim of which was to raise taxes), doubled the representation of the Third Estate (a priori without risk, because voting was by order, and not by head). Many of these representatives were Brethren who travelled for long periods, staying and conversing with other Brethren (sometimes noble ones) along the way. Yet in a society which at the time was still structured rather strictly by caste, it was freedom of speech rather than strength in numbers that may have changed the course of history.

However, we cannot ignore the fact that some reactionary—and then counterrevolutionary—leaders were also Freemasons. One almost too eloquent example is the Duke of Montmorency-Luxembourg. He was General Administrator of the Grand Orient, and the real leader of Masonry before the Revolution, in place of the Duke of Chartres and (subsequently) Duke of Orléans, the constantly absent and later renegade Grand Master. As well as being president of the nobility at the Estates General, Montmorency-Luxembourg was also France's first émigré, leaving on July 15, 1789, and refusing to return.

Finally, there were also Freemasons among both the guillotiners and the guillotined of the Terror. Moreover, the Lodges almost entirely ceased their activities at the start of 1793, only commencing work again after 9 Thermidor: at this stage, they were severely drained. As movement leaders, they were hardly ideal.

Flexible and adaptable, in favor of civil peace and commercial prosperity, just like the business bourgeoisie, Freemasons regrouped under the Directory, the new political regime in France, and quickly showed themselves to be loyalist: their constant doctrine was to comply with the demands of whatever government was in power. In fact, in 1723, this was what Anderson recommended in his *Constitutions*. However, the nineteenth century was a harsh test of this loyalty to the prevailing authorities.

CHAPTER IV
THE RUPTURES OF THE
NINETEENTH CENTURY

I. SITUATION AT THE TURN OF THE CENTURY

O n the cusp of the nineteenth century, the situation of Freemasonry differed considerably between France and England. In terms of numbers, it was prospering in England, with two Grand Lodges, which would soon join to become one. It had a set spirit and customs, huge social prestige, and for over a century, it would accompany the development of the British Empire and (with the Church of England and the monarchy, whose honors and splendor it shared), it would form one of the "three pillars" of English society.

In contrast, in France, emerging from an unprecedented crisis, Lodges were looking for a way forward. This would temporarily be provided by one man: Louis Alexandre Roettiers de Montaleau (1748–1808). This financier from the Ancien Régime was pragmatic and a good negotiator. He united the Lodges under the banner of a still-feeble Grand Orient. He did not become Grand Master (Louis Philippe II, Duke of Orléans, renounced Freemasonry, and was guillotined then not replaced), and took the more modest title of "Grand Venerable." Little by little, work resumed. During the 1780s, the Grand Orient had worked to establish the ritual of its blue (craft) degrees and high degrees, in order to form what came to be called the *Rite Français*. Interrupted by the Revolution, the movement to standardize practices resumed from 1795, and in spite of the irregular circumstances these rituals were published in 1801, in the *Régulateur du maçon* (for blue degrees) and the *Régulateur des Chevaliers Maçons* (for high degrees), works that were to become references.

In 1804, after the Consulate, Bonaparte gained control of the Empire. What would become of Freemasonry in this authoritarian regime? Napoleon, regardless of whether he had or had not been initiated (something that has never been proven), at first considered completely suppressing it. However, he was a keen reader of the English newspapers and thought that Masonry in France could be made into what it was on the other side of the Channel: a backbone for the Empire, which could also honor and reward the elites in order to appease them. This strategy resulted in the astounding rise of French Masonry under the First Empire. In around 1810, at the height of its power, there were over a thousand Lodges, covering much of Europe. Its members included key figures of the Empire, one of the emperor's brothers was Grand Master, and it was directed by the impeccable Cambacérès (1753–1824), Archchancellor of the Empire.

Under such auspices, Masonry was quick to comply. The many prefectural reports of 1811 highlight the peacefulness of the Lodges, filled with "civil servants, peaceable citizens" in the words of the prefect of Gironde. Meanwhile, the prefect of Tarn recorded mostly "known property owners, who are peaceful and incapable of doing or promoting anything against the established order." Nevertheless, the cost of this material prosperity was the almost complete intellectual sterilization of the Masonic Order.

Under Cambacérès, the Grand Orient strived to become the only center of Masonic activity in France, for all degrees. Having merged with the Clermont Grand Lodge in 1799, it gathered and, where necessary, annexed all the different systems of high degrees, forcing them to recognize the authority of the Grand Orient in order to survive. This policy was a success: all the Lodges practicing the French Rite, the Rectified Rite, and the Scottish Philosophical Rite (although these were very marginal), joined the Grand Orient.

At the dawn of the Empire, the Grand Orient de France, with the support of the authorities, and being the institutional if not the moral heir of all eighteenth-century French Masonic experiences, seemed to have gained hegemony among Masons.

However, in 1804, a new return from America shook the French Masonic world.

II. THE TWO FAMILIES OF FRENCH MASONRY IN THE NINETEENTH CENTURY

From 1761, a highly active French Mason, Étienne Morin (1717–1771), endowed with the right to form Lodges by the first Grand Lodge in France, had set up a series of twenty-five degrees in the French Antilles, forming the Ordre du Royal Secret (or the Rite de Perfection). Bringing together the most typical and widespread degrees in Masonic practices of the time, the system had prospered after Morin, and had even gained eight extra degrees, culminating henceforth with that of Sovereign Grand Inspector General. In 1802, a Supreme Council of the 33rd Degree of the Ancient and Accepted Rite (Rite Ancien et Accepté, REAA) was set up in Charleston. It would become the first managing organization for a rite of high degrees with global dimensions. Two years later, a French officer who had left France in 1789, Auguste de Grasse-Tilly, son of a famous admiral, came back to Paris, after the Empire had been proclaimed. He too had an authorization to create a Supreme Council on the French territory.

Faced with the Grand Orient, which at the time was the only power for Lodges of the first three degrees, the Supreme Council initially enlisted the support of a specially created General Scottish Grand Lodge that was based on the same Lodge that had initiated Grasse-Tilly twenty years before. The Philosophical Scottish Rite practiced by this Lodge had since allied itself with the Grand Orient, which allowed it a kind of partial autonomy. Nevertheless, under the inescapable authority of Cambacérès, the young Supreme Council was itself immediately asked to unite with the Grand Orient. A "Concordat" signed in December 1804 gave the Grand Orient power over the first eighteen degrees of the REAA, with the others left to the Supreme Council. However, from 1805, this alliance was broken when the Grand Orient considered it had the right to confer the thirty-third (and last) degree of the Rite as it saw fit. This led to a series of events, but after the confusion surrounding the fall of the Empire, in 1815, Grasse-Tilly's Supreme Council (having theoretically become independent again), could not really practice until after 1821, particularly due to an internal split.

From then on, the Masonic environment was divided until the end of the nineteenth century, with almost constant rivalry between two currents. The first was the Grand Orient, with its numerical majority, practicing the French Rite in its Blue Lodges and holding power over several systems of high degrees. However, around the middle of the century, it practiced almost only those of the REAA itself. It considered itself to be the legitimate heir of the first Supreme Council of France, because of the 1804 Concordat. The second current was the Supreme Council of France, exclusively devoted to the REAA, and which since 1821 had structured a Grande Loge de Commanderie (later becoming a central Grand Lodge), to manage its Blue Lodges of the first three degrees. This was to be the direct ancestor of the current Grand Lodge of France.

Although the philosophical differences were not the same as those seen today, this duality (or rather fraternal rivalry) between the "French Rite" and the "Scottish Rite" has been dominant in French Masonic life since that time.

III. THE 1848 TURNING POINT

The 1830 Revolution had not really pushed French Freemasonry into political action. La Fayette, brought back by circumstances after a long silence under the Empire, and celebrated by all the Lodges as the "hero of the two worlds"—he was a true Masonic icon in his time—had "crowned the Republic" by making the Duke of Orléans king on a balcony of the Paris city hall. Undoubtedly, even a few years earlier, more or less clandestine activist and Republican groups such as those of the *Charbonnerie* (of Italian origin), which were separate from Freemasonry but actually linked to it by members belonging to both, had contributed to social unrest. However, this did not get very far, and this line remained perfectly marginal in a primarily bourgeois Masonry, which was still conformist, as it had been since it began. The 1848 Revolution publicly revealed the political involvement of a significant number of Freemasons.

From March 4, the Grand Orient met in remembrance of the riot victims, and two days later, the interim government received a delegation of Brethren in Masonic decorations at the Paris town hall. It was the minister of justice, Adolphe Crémieux (1796–1880), who answered them on behalf of the interim government. He would later become the Grand Commander of the Supreme Council of France: Masonry was in the street and in power. His statements were not surprising:

> Freemasonry may not have a political objective, but high politics, the politics of humanity, has always found a place in Masonic Lodges. There, in all times and all circumstances, under the oppression of thought and the tyranny of power, Masonry has always repeated those sublime words: *Liberty, Equality, Fraternity.*

Historians might easily question this extremely imaginative analysis, and would struggle to find proof to support it in the Masonic historiography of the preceding century. However, it showed a new mindset, which concerned French Masonry as a whole, not forgetting the great ambiguity of the in many ways romantic and almost mystical revolution of 1848. Sometimes, the roles were reversed: whereas a national Grand Lodge of France (a breakoff of the Supreme Council) created such agitation in 1851 that it was subsequently banned by the chief of police, in 1849 the Grand Orient de France introduced the obligation to believe in God and the immortal soul into its Constitution.

However, the government's program was heavily influenced by the progressive ideas of some Brethren, particularly Victor Schœlcher (1804–1893), who obtained the abolition of slavery. The coup d'état of December 2, 1851, allowed the Grand Orient, which was perpetually legalist and somewhat nostalgic for the First Empire (except for a few irredentist Lodges), to elect the Prince Murat as Grand Master. However, in 1862 Marshall Magnan, the coup d'état's sabreur, succeeded him on the emperor's wishes. The Supreme Council, stunned to be under his authority, proudly resisted him. The duality thus continued.

The intellectual and political transformation of French Freemasonry (in all Obediences) was undoubtedly completed under the authoritarian years of the Second Empire (1852–1860). Towards the end of the regime, the Republican Party, deprived of any legal existence, largely identified itself with the apparatus provided by the network of Masonic Lodges across the whole territory, again with all their contradictions and different social strata.

It is clear how far the evolution of Freemasonry in France was essentially linked to its political and social history. No such phenomenon was seen in Great Britain, for example, which remained the historical center of the Order. There, since the start of the nineteenth century at least, the Masonic institution had been completely integrated into the power structures and aligned with the social norm.

IV. THE CHURCH OF THE REPUBLIC

After March 18, 1871, and the outbreak of the Paris Commune, Paris's Masons became definitively involved. Many revolutionary officials were Masons, for example Jules Vallès and Élisée Reclus. However, so were many partisans of reconciliation with Versailles, such as Charles Floquet. They all took part in the great demonstration on April 29, where several hundreds of Masons from both Obediences and dozens of different Lodges marched in front of the national guards for several hours.

After this Parisian revolution (the provincial Lodges remained largely in favor of reconciliation), Masonry would long remain at the front line of the Republican struggle.

The spiritualist proclamation introduced into the Constitution of the Grand Orient, in the elation of 1848, was subject to growing opposition from many Lodges in the 1860s. A request at the 1875 and 1876 congresses for the removal of the obligation to believe in God and the immortal soul was finally discussed in 1877. The decision was unproblematic, and the proposal was adopted with a large majority. The Grand Orient thus completed an evolution that had begun at least fifty years earlier. It now professed strict agnosticism, and therefore did not in principle condemn any belief. The United Grand Lodge of England, for reasons that were at least as much geopolitical as they were purely Masonic, used this as an argument to break off its relations with the Grand Orient, which in any case had never been formally established. Nevertheless, at the time, the close connections between the "priest party" and the enemies of the Republic, which became clear with the Dreyfus Affair (1894-1906), would for several decades bring Freemasonry as a whole into often violent conflict with the high Catholic clergy.

In fact, although the Grand Orient had been in the foreground since 1870, the Lodges of the Supreme Council did not remain untouched by the general evolution. Although the Lausanne Congress of Supreme Councils of 1875 had reaffirmed the existence of a "Creative Principle" (among much more progressive but often forgotten commitments), in France in 1876 the Grand Commander Crémieux nevertheless had to reaffirm that the Supreme Council gave "no form" to the Great Architect of the Universe. In this period, the power of the high degrees was no less seriously contested by the Blue Lodges.

In 1880, twelve Lodges left the Supreme Council to form the Grande Loge Symbolique Écossaise (Symbolic Scottish Grand Lodge). This Lodge was resolutely democratic in its operations, libertarian in its mindset, and hostile towards the high degrees, and it had ties to feminism. Its members included Masons with a great future, such as Gustave Mesureur (1847–1925), an eminent member of the Radical Party who later became Grand Master of the Grande Loge de France (Grand Lodge of France). Under ongoing pressure from its sixty Blue Lodges, the Supreme Council eventually granted them independence in 1894. Two years later, the merger with the thirty-six Lodges that made up the Grande Loge Symbolique (Symbolic Grand Lodge) at the time was confirmed, thus definitively creating the Grande Loge de France.

For at least three decades, until the law separating the French state from the Church (which was its soul) under the ministry of Émile Combes (1835–1921), who had been a Mason since 1869, Freemasonry appeared and above all considered itself to be one of the key bastions of the Republican and secular battle. Its very strong links with French radicalism made this radicalism into a sort of political showcase for Freemasonry. As such, around a third of Lodges joined the founding congress of the Radical Republican Party in 1901.

CHAPTER V
THE FORTUNES AND MISFORTUNES OF FREEMASONRY IN THE TWENTIETH CENTURY

Unfortunately, it is not possible here to give a detailed account of Freemasonry's rich and complex history in a century that saw an unprecedented number of Freemasons in the world, in Europe, and above all in France.[10] We will therefore focus on just two periods.

I. THE PREWAR PERIOD

Despite its European "network" and humanitarian principles, Freemasonry did not prevent war: neither that of 1870, nor that of 1914, and certainly not that of 1939. It could not rival Hitler or Mussolini. It was brutally pursued in totalitarian countries and almost completely disappeared in Germany, Italy, Spain, Portugal, and countries that were occupied by Germany. Soviet Russia was no more favorable.

In France, throughout the entire Third Republic, Freemasonry exerted moral authority against the "priest party" and the fascist leagues. With all Obediences almost entirely identified with the secular battle, it took on all the associated risks: that of losing a part of its initial vocation, as well as that of suffering the terrible vengeance of its enemies when they came to power following the defeat of June 1940. Marshal Pétain was even more anti-Masonic than he was anti-Semitic. Tellingly, the laws banning Obediences were even published before the text against the Jews. French Freemasonry was therefore almost wiped out, going from thirty-five

---

10   For a more exhaustive approach to the modern and contemporary period, see Roger Dachez, *Histoire de la franc-maçonnerie française* (Paris: Puf, 2003).

thousand Brothers in the Grand Orient in 1939 to fewer than six thousand in 1945. The proportions were identical for the whole French Masonic context, and for both the Grand Lodge and the new Independent and Regular National Grand Lodge (which in 1948 became the Grande Loge Nationale Française, or French National Grand Lodge), an affiliate of London in France that was born in 1913 out of a division of two Lodges practicing the Rectified Rite of the Grand Orient de France.

Primarily concerned with its external activities, Masonry nevertheless succeeded after the First World War in facilitating the creation of the League of Nations through the Treaty of Versailles in 1919, based on an idea from the Brother Léon Bourgeois that was adopted by the Freemason American president Woodrow Wilson. Thanks to the "questions studied by the Lodges," the Freemasons also began to rethink society. However, they did not always do so in a very practical way: one of their last ideas before the Second World War was the aim of disarmament. Nor was their thinking very popular: from the 1920s they had also recommended the adoption of proportional and progressive income tax.

Amid the debris of victory, and with a return to peace, everything needed to be rebuilt.

II. THE IMMEDIATE POSTWAR PERIOD

The impact of the persecution under the Occupation brought a significant change of direction in French Masonic thought. The Freemasons questioned the way in which they had been bogged down in political and social life for decades, abandoned their rituals, and forgotten their tradition. For several months, they dreamed of a union between the two "enemy brothers" (the Grand Orient and the Grande Loge), but from 1945, this dream faded. Nevertheless, the French Masonic landscape underwent a progressive and profound restructuring.

In 1945, the Lodges adopted by the Grande Loge de France were set "free," allowing the creation of the Women's Masonic Union of France, which in 1959 became the Women's Grand Lodge of France. This was the first women's Obedience in the world and increasingly grew in importance.

Splits occurred: in 1958, a departure from the Grande Loge Nationale Française gave rise to the Grande Loge Traditionnelle et Symbolique Opéra. Conversely, in 1965, a small minority of Brothers from the Grande Loge de France left this Obedience to join the Grande Loge Nationale Française. The Supreme Council of France, governing the high degrees of the Ancient and Accepted Scottish Rite, also split, and this division remains today. Although all of these conflicts were separate, they concerned similar issues: regularity and tradition.

Everywhere, Masons felt a need to return to the observance of traditional rituals and focus on Masonic work, without moral and spiritual definition. Some also felt that returning to "international regularity" was the best way of achieving this, whereas others did not think it necessary. From the 1970s, the context became even more complex, with the appearance of several more Obediences, which often had few members and generally remained modest or disappeared within a few years. The compulsive fission of French Masonry intensified, and it shaped the face of Freemasonry in France today.

III. CONTEMPORARY ISSUES

Today, Masonry in France attracts hordes of young and socially engaged men and women, but also new social groups, such as the recent generations of immigrant descent, for whom it can play a valuable role in terms of Republican integration. All of these members bring the questions and expectations—the hopes and demands—of their time. This flourishing is undoubtedly a mark of vigor, dynamism, and originality. It is also very clearly a seed of disorder, and presents risks of confusion within Masonry, of its image moving to the Left, and of its influence being weakened.

Nevertheless, compared to the international context, French Freemasonry is in a strong position. At its 1950s peak, American Masonry had almost four million Brothers, but had hardly more than two million at the start of the 2000s, only a small percentage of whom were still active. British Masonry had almost a million members, but has less than five hundred thousand today. In contrast, in France, Belgium, and the eastern countries, there is still a strong dynamic. Today, there are almost 150,000 Brothers and Sisters in the French mainland and overseas territories, out of a total 2.5 to 3 million Masons in the world, with the traditional Anglo-Saxon strongholds falling inexorably.

Three centuries on, the tale continues . . .

PART TWO

THE MASONIC WORLD

CHAPTER VI
SYMBOLS

One of the most striking traits of the Masonic world, for anyone approaching it from a "profane" point of view, is the number and range of two- and three- dimensional symbols that populate Lodges and are worn by Freemasons: in France, they say that they "decorate" themselves during their work. This is the custom that both surprises and interests people the most, but it also causes mockery, or at least severe incomprehension. It can be hard to know where the boundary lies between an unusual and disconcerting way of passing down teachings, which is enigmatic, if not secret, and the outdated and vaguely upsetting remnant of social customs from another age.

I. THE SOURCES OF MASONIC SYMBOLS

1. **The Symbolic Foundations of European Culture.** It is useful to begin this section by correcting a common misconception, namely that there are specific symbols belonging uniquely to the Masonic world and produced exclusively for use by Freemasons. Nothing could be further from the truth. Most (if not all) so-called "Masonic" symbols come from various sources, often dating very far back in Western culture, which are above all nothing to do with the world of Craft Guilds.

This poses the question of whether it is possible to glimpse the outline of a symbolic teaching in the tradition of builders, even in the Middle Ages.

The difficulty here is the lack of sources. In the first instance, we can only refer to the *Old Charges*, the oldest of which date back (as we have seen) to the end of the fourteenth century. These documents offer a legendary and mythical history of the Craft, but contain no hint of symbolic discourse. They talk of geometry as if it is identified with Masonry, and cite Euclid and Pythagoras, which seems very erudite for a medieval guilds of artisans.

It is therefore necessary to refer to other sources, which are admittedly very limited. Still, there is at least one worth citing: the famous square found at the end of the nineteenth century in Limerick, Ireland, during work to rebuild an old bridge dating back to the sixteenth century that was threatening to collapse. In the northeast column of the bridge, buried in its mass, a metal square was found. Written on it was: "I will strive to live with love and care upon the level, by the square," and a date: "1507."

This short phrase is obviously remarkable. It is an admittedly isolated example, but nevertheless a very strong and even rather moving one, which shows that in fifteenth- or sixteenth-century Ireland workers had already attributed moral and spiritual meaning to some of their tools. There must have been other cases of this rather simple but very eloquent and even rather "natural" moral symbolism. It is therefore possible that even in the Middle Ages, men were already seeing hidden meanings in their tools, embodied by their shapes or everyday use. The case for accepting this source is all the more compelling because it uncontestably corresponds to the "analogical" mentality of the period, of which there are many other examples in numerous other domains, starting with medicine or quite simply popular magic of the time. It is conceivable that it may have been talked of on construction sites, like a sort of folklore of the Craft. However, nothing, no document, allows us to assert that such analogies were part of a structured teaching, especially not the major teaching delivered in the secrecy of supposed medieval Lodges, among other marvelous secrets like geometry or the art of tracing.

Thus, we must propose lines of investigation other than just the "natural" symbolism of the profession, which is all in all rather disappointing.

Beyond a supposed "secret teaching" of builders, we must therefore remember that throughout the Middle Ages there was a symbolic theology engraved in the stone of almost all religious buildings, because there was a key for interpreting the sacred writings. This typological thought was, in principle, nothing more than the application of symbolism to history. As has long been shown in the still-fascinating studies of Émile Mâle,[11] this thought has left us a veritable stone Bible. At a time when almost nobody could read, the many sculpted figures followed precise norms, leaving little room for artistic freedom. They were based on a deep, faithful, and didactic analysis of Christian doctrine, for which churches and to an even greater extent, cathedrals, had to be open books. This tangle of symbols is filled, for example, with triangles referring to the Trinity, while the square frequently appears among the traditional symbols allowing reliable identification of the saints (James the Less, Matthew, Thomas the Apostle, Joseph the Carpenter).

Not only is this a reliable source, but we can retrace its transmission in Masonic tradition, which at the time was still being formed: it should be remembered that building sites were managed by clerics, who directed the work and provided moral and spiritual supervision for the workers. It was one such cleric who wrote the *Regius* manuscript, the oldest known version of the *Old Charges*.

However, although the contribution of religious thought and the Church as a teaching body did play a major role in the formation of the symbolic and traditional corpus of Masonry, it cannot explain everything.

---

11   See in particular Émile Mâle, *L'Art religieux au XIIIe siècle. Étude sur les origines de l'iconographie du Moyen Âge et sur ses sources d'inspiration* (Paris: Armand Colin, 1948 and several new editions).

Incontestably, another notable stage in its development was Renaissance thinking. This is our third source, already mentioned more generally above. It clearly attributed a new meaning to architecture, and contributed to the emergence of a new intellectual type: the architect.

Drawing upon Vitruvian tradition going back to the first century AD, which had already made the architect a man of universal knowledge and multiple talents, the most influential Renaissance authors added a finishing touch to this ideal portrait. One such case, which will be examined later in this book, was the French architect Philibert de l'Orme (1510–1570). Others, such as Serlio, even offered more precise indications, by describing what must be considered as a symbolic interpretation of the orders of architecture.

The interest of the Renaissance intellectual mutation within the architectural domain goes beyond just a history of art and techniques. Disturbingly, elements of a speculative, architecture-based discourse can be identified, showing great similarity with what would, towards the end of the seventeenth century, be the symbolic method of Speculative Freemasonry.

From the end of the sixteenth century, this new view of architecture and the architect's role was perfectly familiar in England. Hence, certain very old ideas were undergoing a revival. For example, the idea that God's work of creation was similar to the work of an architect or a geometrist can be traced back to Plato himself. In the origins of the Renaissance at the end of the fifteenth century, Pico della Mirandola saw God as the "most talented of artisans." Johannes Valentinus Andreae, in his utopia entitled *Christianopolis* (1619), represented God as the "Supreme Architect." Such an image was therefore very common in this period, and can also be seen in 1630, with the writings of English doctor and Christian moralist Sir Thomas Browne, who uses the expression "High Architect of the World."

One source of inspiration for the phrase was, perhaps, Calvin himself, who almost a century earlier in his *Commentary on Psalm 19* (1557) wrote that the heavens had been "wonderfully created by the eminent artisan" [*ab opifice praestantissimo*]. Earlier we evoked the striking example of emblematic literature. We could also add that of architectural treatises, which proliferated first in Italy from the fifteenth century, then in France in the sixteenth century. The most famous of these in France, Philibert de l'Orme's *Les Dix Livres de l'Architecture* (*The Ten Books on Architecture*), was published in 1567. However, it is in the *Epsitre aux lecteurs* that God is described as "grand and admirable Architect of the universal world," for the first time in French, while book 1 of the same work, amid purely technical considerations, includes what can be seen as a discourse on the symbolism of the cross.

Philibert de l'Orme: a Speculative Freemason in France, right in the middle of the sixteenth century? Not by any stretch of the imagination. Nevertheless, it is clear that his interpretive view of geometrical figures, with its religious and spiritual tone, was already a natural component of the broad universalist vision, which in Renaissance thought, over a century before the first manifestations of Speculative Masonry, attributed a culture of multiple harmonies to the architect.

The intellectual climate of the Renaissance was therefore undeniably the melting pot in which (outside of any direct connection with the masonry craft) a way of thinking based on analogical connections in the moral or spiritual domain developed. Once again, it is necessary to emphasize the great importance the abundant literature of the *emblemata*, the enigmatic plates without commentary that filled many works throughout the sixteenth and seventeenth centuries. The exercise that they propose, of meditation and interiorization of a coded message, with the many "future Masonic symbols" seen in the illustrations (the compass, the square, the plumb line), is undoubtedly another surprising foreshadowing of the intellectual method adopted by early Speculative Masonry.

Similarly, as emphasized by the works of Frances Yates mentioned above, we must acknowledge the importance of "the art of memory," a method inherited from antiquity and rediscovered in the Middle Ages, which allowed orators to remember the meanderings of their speeches by connecting them in their minds with the rooms of an ideal abode, which they would visit in their mind as they spoke. The intellectual circles of the Renaissance also adopted this method, but focused on the idea that visualizing a space or building could allow an intellectual journey. Finally, the remarkable works of the Scottish historian David Stevenson[12] established undeniable links between this intellectual tradition and the environments structuring the Lodges in Scotland at the end of the seventeenth century. The main customs of these were adopted by British Speculative Masonry several decades later.

Later (and we will not dwell on this last source, which has been the subject of much study), the contributions of Hermeticism, already mentioned above, and much later of neochivalry, laid the final stones.

2. The Composition of the Symbolic Repertoire of Freemasonry. Although the elements of the symbolic repertoire of Freemasonry are not original, it was nevertheless not created in a day: it is the product of many successive and not necessarily concerted contributions. This explains the extraordinarily varied and recurrent, or in some cases heterogeneous and sometimes contradictory symbols, across the diverse rites and traditions of different countries. Looking at the oldest known Masonic rituals (from Scotland at the end of the seventeenth century), we can observe the relative dearth of symbolic material. There are essentially just a few stones and tools, some

12   David Stevenson, *The Origins of Freemasonry: Scotland's Century, 1590-1710* (Cambridge: Cambridge University Press, 1990).

of which later disappeared from Masonic symbolism. However, the "major symbols" like the triangle, the compass, and the square are clearly absent.

There are no other really usable documents until those from the mid-1720s in Great Britain. However, in revelations and the first published rituals (Prichard, *Masonry Dissected*, 1730), the "toolbox" of the Speculative Freemasons is considerably larger. It was almost complete when the first printed revelations came out in France (*Le Secret des francs-maçons*, 1744), as shown by the beautiful images in the works. From then on, it hardly changed. Crossing the Channel to France, with miscomprehensions and mistranslations, some symbols were even "invented" and are not used by English Freemasons today. Examples include the "pointed cubic stone" ("Pierre cubique à pointe" - a perfectly functioning deviation) and the "serrated tassel" ("Houppe dentelée" - a completely meaningless expression).

The symbols and objects of Solomon's Temple (the altar of perfumes, the seven-branched candlestick, and the Ark of the Covenant) did not enter Masonic rituals until the 1740s or later, with the first high degrees gradually introduced after the 1730s. As for the Hermetic and alchemical symbols, these came much later, only appearing between 1750 and 1760. In contrast, in these same degrees, the references to the purely Masonic and operative world would become rarer.

Therefore, according to how one interprets it, it took thirty to fifty years in the first half of the eighteenth century for the stable set of Masonic symbols to form.

II. SYMBOLS IN MASONIC THOUGHT AND PRACTICE

1. The Main Masonic Symbols. This is not the place to comment on the different symbols found in the various degrees and rites within Freemasonry. There is abundant literature on this subject, of highly variable quality, which is the main reference for the thought of certain Freemasons, and the direct source on which they drew to pad out the "plates" sometimes presented in Lodges.

Here, we will content ourselves with a nonexhaustive but structured list. The Masonic world uses various kinds of symbols:

- *objects directly linked to the practice of the masonry craft*: the mallet, the chisel, the level, the plumb line, and the trowel;

- *materials from the art of building*: the rough stone and the cubic stone;

- *architectural elements*: plans, orders of architecture, and various arches and vaults;

- *mathematical instruments*, particularly ones for geometry and not used by builders, such as the square and the compass;

- *astronomical symbols*: the sun, the moon, and the stars;

- *alchemical symbols*: salt and mercury;

- *universal symbols* (generally simple geometrical shapes given religious significance in different traditions): the point, the cross, the circle, and the triangle;

- *initial letters used as symbols*: the tenth letter of the Hebrew alphabet and first letter of the tetragrammaton, *yod*, or the tetragrammaton as a whole, and the letter G (the first letter of "geometry," but also of "God");

- *elements borrowed from the Bible*, particularly Solomon's Temple: the columns J and B and the "mosaic" pavement, the seven-branched (but also three-, five-, or nine-branched) candlestick, the Ark of the Covenant, and even the Tower of Babel;

- *symbols whose name or form are specific to Freemasonry*: the "serrated tassel", the "pointed cubic stone". These are the least numerous.

It is natural to link these symbols to what French Freemasons call their "decorations"- and English speaking ones, *regalia*. These word refer not only to the elements adorning their meeting places precisely to give them symbolic meaning, but above all to the specific items of clothing that they wear and that indicate their functions, degrees, and dignities. These include collars, ribbons (often with symbolic jewels), gloves, headgear, and of course the dagger or sword with its indispensable belt, and finally aprons in all shapes, sizes, and colors (which are symbols in themselves): white, blue, red, green, and black, with yellow, orange, brown, and violet being rarer in Masonic decorations. These in turn are decorated with many shapes and images.

This eclectic list obviously calls for reflection. Nevertheless, we should not waste time searching for some coherent origin connecting these disparate elements, even if there are clear links between some of them. They are the result of a gradual accumulation over the decades and centuries, according to the (sometimes admirable) fancies and imaginations of the authors of rituals and creators of degrees, but also of the anonymous masses of "unknown Masons without degree" from different places and periods, who successfully introduced new objects for reasons and circumstances that are still a mystery to us.

We must simply observe and accept as an essential fact that this symbolic world is an integral part of Freemasonry, and that without it, Freemasonry would lose all specificity (if not all meaning), and the very principle of its existence. More precisely, without its symbols and the dynamism that they bring, Freemasonry would be nothing more (depending on the place and period) than a simple mutual-aid association, a philosophical circle, a fraternal community, or even a "service club," a political lobby, or an influence network. In France, it has, over time, been all of these things, separately or in combination.

The important thing is to understand that Freemasons have always placed the use of symbols at the heart of their institution. In France, it has often even been called "the symbolic method." Yet although there is almost unanimous agreement as to the importance of this tool, it is far from certain that they all see and apply it in the same way.

Masonic symbolism, or what is referred to as such, when examined with a degree of distance, seems to contain many ambiguities.

2. The Ambiguity of Symbolic Thought. According to William Preston (1742–1818), an author deeply revered by English Freemasons, who in the last quarter of the eighteenth century, particularly through his masterpiece, *Illustrations of Masonry*, contributed to the fixing of rituals and instructions that are still used in British Lodges today, Freemasonry is "a system of morality, veiled in allegory, and illustrated by symbols." Whether or not we agree with this definition, it is one of the oldest that Freemasonry has left us of its symbolic method. For this, at least, it is worthy of consideration. However, there are two particularly striking terms: "morality" and "illustrated." In this perspective, although Freemasonry is typically Anglo-Saxon, it above all teaches "the sacred principles of morality," as expressly stated by the ritual of initiation to the first degree in England, and only uses symbols as a convenient and suggestive means of "illustrating" this teaching. In Preston's time, throughout the nineteenth century, and to this day, British Freemasonry has continued to see Masonic symbols as simple emblems which serve as graphic reminders of the fundamental teachings of Judeo-Christian morality, the foundations of which can be found in the sacred writings. According to the English rituals, these are "unfailing criteria for justice and truth."

But what of France, particularly in the eighteenth century? The word *symbol* was rarely (and in certain systems, almost never) used in Masonic rituals and discourses. As in Great Britain, the words *allegories* and *emblems*, or even *hieroglyphs* and *types* are more commonly seen. However, from the very beginning, the French Masonic vocabulary has made abundant use of one particular word: *secret*, generally in the plural.

The first French Masonic disclosures, by their very titles, express this mindset: *Le Secret des francs-maçons* (*The Secret of the Freemasons* 1744), *Le Sceau rompu* (*The Broken Seal*, 1745), *L'Ordre des francs-maçons trahi et leur secret révélé* (*The Order of the Freemasons Betrayed, and their Secret Revealed*, 1745). Again, these revelations concerned only the first three degrees (the "blue" degrees or "symbolic" degrees). However, from 1766 these printed indiscretions also targeted the high degrees. The most celebrated work on this issue was entitled *Les Plus Secrets mystères des hauts grades de la maçonnerie dévoilés* (*The Most Secret Mysteries of the High Degrees of Masonry Revealed*). Clearly, compared to the English "symbolic illustration," these expressions strongly imply that Freemasonry, connected to the oldest "tradition of mysteries," possesses teachings that are carefully protected from profane curiosity, and that the symbols used by Freemasons aim not to illustrate, but to hide and disguise the great truths that the order dispenses to its members.

At the end of the nineteenth century, particularly in France, within the occultist current started by Éliphas Lévi (alias Alphonse Louis Constant, 1810–1875) that was close to Freemasonry (itself mainly positivist at the time), a very particular hermeneutic current slowly gained ground. Towards the end of the 1950s, if not dominant, it was at least unavoidable in Masonic thought in general. This movement was indisputably launched by Oswald Wirth (1860–1943), a pupil of the esotericist and somewhat inflammatory Stanislas de Guaïta (1861–1897). From 1890, he published his highly famous *La Franc-maçonne rendue intelligible à ses adeptes* (*Freemasonry Explained to Its Followers*) in three volumes: I. *L'Apprenti* (*The Apprentice*), II. *Le Compagnon* (*The Fellowcraft*), and

III. *Le Maître* (*The Master*). These were followed by *Les Mystères de l'art royal* (*The Mysteries of the Royal Art*). The works were soon translated into several languages (but not English: titles and quotations are translated here for the purposes of this analysis). Thus, for over forty years, Wirth committed himself to studying Masonic symbols and editing his aptly titled journal, *Le Symbolisme* (launched en 1912). This publication continued after his death, until 1970.

Through his works, which are written in classical and clear language, and which, in the words of their author, are real "Masonic handbooks," Wirth imposed his concise vision in a few short formulae:

> Profane science is taught through words, whereas the initiatory knowledge can only be acquired through symbols. The Initiate finds this wisdom (*gnosis* in Greek) within himself, by discerning subtle allusions. He must look for what lies hidden in the depths of his mind. . . .

> Faced with an unspeaking sign, the follower must make it speak: *thinking for oneself* is the great art of Members.

Les Mystères de l'art royal

In terms of influence and in the same vein, only Jules Boucher is really comparable. This other twentieth-century occultist, magician, and theurgist wrote *La Symbolique maçonnique* (*Masonic Symbology*), a work published for the first time in 1948, which was (and is to this day) a real bestseller in French Lodges.

From a moralizing rebus, Masonic symbology thus became the tool in a real spiritual exercise, with rather Illuminist or mystic connotations. Nevertheless, this "symbolist" approach also had unspoken elements, which we will not dwell on too much here. Referring to much more metaphysical than simply moral questions (unlike the somewhat basic symbolism of the English tradition), this French Masonic symbolism also stands out for its extreme reluctance to invoke any overly direct religious reference. Revealingly, Wirth himself, an enthusiastic prophet of the "symbolist renewal" of Freemasonry who readily used astrology, tarot, or alchemy as keys for understanding Masonic symbols, had always interpreted the traditional "vocabulary" of the "Grand Architect of the Universe" (an image unequivocally designating God among English Freemasons) as a "pure symbol." In other words, as anything except God, or at least just as lip service.

The French version of Masonic symbolism therefore appeared rather late in the history of Freemasonry, although some of its roots can be traced back to certain minor rites from the end of the eighteenth century. The word "symbolism" in the Masonic context thus became buried in a certain semantic haze. In the mouths of some of its defenders and critics within Lodges, it even became a euphemistic equivalent of spiritualism or Deism: a person was a "symbolist Mason" and that said it all. Consequently, there was a subtle and unspoken move from the simple designation of a method to the affirmation of an intellectual position and almost a metaphysical choice: this was obviously a big difference.

Even in this case, however, and according to another very common acceptation in French Masonic circles, the "symbolic" nature was still connected to freedom of imagination and conscience, without necessarily referring to any "dogmatic" assertion.

This typically French interspace shows how far the cultural context influences the reception and treatment of a corpus of symbols, which have the same general morphology everywhere. Later in this study, we will attempt to identify the sources, nature, and extent of this ultimate ambiguity, by examining the links between Masonry, religion, and esotericism.

CHAPTER VII
RITUALS

R ites and rituals are closely linked to symbols. In the words of René Guénon (1886–1951), a highly influential exegete in certain French Masonic circles today:

> First of all, it can be said that the symbol, seen as a "graphic" representation, as it most commonly is, in some ways is nothing more than the fixing of a ritual gesture. The drawing of the symbol sometimes even needs to be carried out in conditions that give it all the characteristics of a rite.[13]

We might debate the direction of the connection evoked here (rite → symbol or symbol → rite), but the connection itself is undeniable. Moreover, the feeling of strangeness experienced by the neophyte observer when told of "Masonic rites" is similar to his or her perplexity when faced with the symbols that decorate the temples of the Sons and Daughters of the Light.

I. RITUALS: AN ANTHROPOLOGICAL CONSTANT

However, this apparent strangeness is only explained by an evolution which, in modern Western countries, has gradually eliminated most of the social rites that punctuated the daily lives of European peoples for many centuries. The advances in cultural anthropology over the last century have revealed a real constant of the human condition. In his still-famous and informative work, *The Rites of Passage* (1909), Arnold Van Gennep, also the author of a monumental *Manual of Contemporary French Folklore*,

---

13   René Guénon, *"Le Rite et le symbole," in Aperçus sur l'initiation* (Paris: Édi-tions traditionnelles, 1946).

showed the close links (both in form and content) between the puberty rites that have existed since time immemorial in Africa or in Oceania on the one hand, and many popular rural customs that only fully disappeared during the nineteenth century, still leaving many visible traces today.

With specific regard to the European context in which Freemasonry was born, from the Middle Ages and over the centuries all the social behaviors and major acts of civil life (as much as religious life) had been punctuated by symbolic acts and rituals. This permanent symbolization of life gave it meaning and affected everyone, with the same patterns occurring in all social strata: from the arming of a knight to the reception of a fellow of a craft, to the consecration of a bishop or the installation of a county magistrate, across the whole scale of human conditions, everything had to follow the order of the world, which was always somewhat sacred.

Today, there are few statuses or professions that require the accomplishment of symbolic acts such as a solemn vow in order to rise to a new function or degree (in France, the famous "Hippocratic Oath" of new doctors in medicine, before their masters in their gowns, is one of the ultimate examples of this type of act). This is why the major ritualization of Freemasonry, today equaled only by that of religions, seems so strange to us. Hardly three centuries ago, it was not so surprising.

But why all these rituals and ceremonies, when simple words or a few documents are enough to emphasize the sense of a responsibility, a status, or the passage to a new stage in life?

The answer to such a question is not specifically Masonic. It belongs to the conjoined domains of ethnology, sociology, depth psychology or analytical psychology, and the comparative history of religions. Jean Cazeneuve, in an inspired thesis, expressed this problem very well:

It is not possible to define the function of the rite as a substitute for instinct or a neurotic process, or even as a sacralization of the social phenomenon, because there will always be rites that do not fit any one of these assimilations. In truth, rites are complex and even contradictory phenomena. One might even say they are dialectical. A rite both seeks an antithesis and attempts to overcome it. Society, by obeying what M. Davy calls an "instinct of the rule," aims for an ideal of absolute conditioning. However, man naturally has a taste for freedom and the unconditioned. The human condition defined by rules is opposed by the numinous,[14] a source of both fear and power... The rite is a ransom of man's individual autonomy, a defense reaction triggered by the feeling that he might become lost by becoming too imprisoned in his role or by escaping too far from himself.[15]

Freemasonry has therefore taken the elements of its rituals from this fundamental source at the very heart of man's nature, and not from some outdated fantasy: as we have already seen, they also come from other, more contingent sources, linked to the cultural history of Europe after the Renaissance.

II. A SHORT HISTORY OF MASONIC RITUALS

There is no doubt that ritual acts have been carried out within the building professions, on building sites or elsewhere, since medieval times. Were they in any way linked to those seen in Speculative Masonry today? Nothing could be less certain, and we have never seen any documents that might prove such a hypotheses. As for the fellowship rituals seen today, these are precisely the result of a massive contamination by Masonic

---

14   This is a key concept borrowed from Rudolf Otto's *The Idea of the Holy,* originally published as *Das Heilige* (1917): the feeling of an unknowable phenomenon beneath everything, which both exalts (*mysterium fascinans*) and disturbs (*mysterium tremendum*).

15   Jean Cazeneuve, *Les Rites et la condition humaine* (Paris: Puf, 1958).

customs that emerged during the nineteenth century. Consequently, they cannot be used as a source.

Since the fifteenth century, the *Old Charges* have told us that a history of the profession was read to the young apprentice, and that (at least towards the end of the sixteenth century) this apprentice made a vow, for which we have the text. This is both useful and insufficient. For their part, the English "accepted Masons" of the second half of the seventeenth century whose names have been passed down to us by history, including the famous Elias Ashmole (1617–1692), told nothing of the Masonic customs revealed to them. However, once again, it seems that a manuscript of the *Old Rites* was read, and that there was a vow with a few practical secrets (words allowing recognition, and hand signals). However, there are still huge gaps in the information. In fact, the oldest known Masonic rituals clearly deserving of this name go back to the very last years of the seventeenth century, and the first two decades of the eighteenth century, and are of Scottish origin.

Four manuscripts, written between around 1696 to around 1715, provide evidence of this, revealing the form and content of this "early" Freemasonry. We will now examine its essential traits.

At the time, the Masonic career, if we can call it this, included only two "grades" (the term most commonly used in French) or "degrees" (a word that only appeared in Masonic custom in 1730): the Entered Apprentice and the Fellowcraft. The ceremonies were very simple and short. The Lodge was overseen by a Warden or a *Praeses* that had only one (not two) assessors. No tracing board in the center of the Lodge is mentioned, but three candlesticks arranged in a triangle are described. When initiated (the word was not yet used, and the commonly used phrase was "to make a Mason") the candidate was received blindfold, entered giving three distinct knocks, circled the Lodge three times, then made his vow, and received the secrets (words and signs or gestures allowing recognition). For the following degree, the ceremony was essentially a greeting in the form of a mutual embrace, with the main postures corresponding to the Five Points of Fellowship (which were later transferred to the Master degree when it became distinct).

Various printed and handwritten revelations from 1724–1725, this time in England, recount the essentials of this schema. Samuel Prichard's great revelation, *Masonry Dissected*, published in 1730 and the subject of much scandal, is not strictly speaking a ritual, but rather a commented Masonic catechism (a "teaching in the form of questions and answers"). It shows that Masonic practice in London from 1720 to 1730 reproduced these Scottish customs, with some adjustments and developments. The main development was the individualization of a new degree: that of Master Mason.

Prichard's revelation gives us, for the first time, the account of the death of the Master Hiram (represented since 1723 in James Anderson's *Constitutions* as the architect of Solomon's Temple, although the Bible does not state this), and the relationship between this tragic event and the degree of Master Mason. The "Master's Word" (which, according to legend, was a secret known to Hiram, King Solomon, and King Hiram of Tyre) is replaced by a substitute word with the initials "M.B.," several forms of which are mentioned in various texts from the same period. The Five Points of Fellowship serve to reveal the Master who replaces Hiram in the course of the elevation ceremony. In the second degree, left almost without symbolic and ritual content because of this transfer, the letter G (for *God* or *geometry*), is of central importance.

The symbolic landmarks and key rituals of the first three degrees were thus established, between Scotland and England, from the end of the seventeenth century to the 1720s. After this, they hardly changed, and the first summary given by Prichard (that circulated by the first Grand

Lodge of London, founded in 1717 and later called the Grand Lodge of the "Moderns") therefore expresses the oldest documented Masonic practice. This practice was the one that came to France in around 1725 at the latest. No more new elements were introduced until the 1750s.

This was when the second symbolic and ritual tradition appeared: that of the Ancient Grand Lodge, created in London by Irish immigrants between 1751 and 1753. It constitutes a founding custom, along with the first of all the Masonic customs known to this day. Undoubtedly coming from England to Ireland at the end of the seventeenth century, there was Masonic activity in Dublin in 1688. However, in still almost entirely unknown circumstances, there was an autonomous and specific evolution of the system of the Ancients, known to us due to a very well-written ritual, printed in London in 1760 and entitled *The Three Distinct Knocks*. All of the ceremonies for the first three degrees follow an almost identical pattern to that of the Moderns' system, including the degree of Master Mason that appeared among the Moderns in London. However, the symbolic landmarks of the Ancients differ in several ways: the attribution of the names J (Jakhin) and B (Boaz) to the two columns of the Temple follows a reversed order, and the two Wardens are placed to the west by the Moderns, but to the south (for the second Warden) and the west (for the first Warden) by the Ancients. The three large candlesticks, which for the Moderns have since at least the mid-1730s surrounded a symbolic tracing board on the floor of the Lodge, are arranged differently by the Ancients, who do not use a board.

Outside of the 1753–1813 historical conflict between the two rival Grand Lodges of England, which eventually ended with their fusion, the duality of symbolic systems described above served as a reminder that all Masonic rites (the specific and variable ways of working the first three degrees) are part of one of these two traditions. In France, for example, the oldest and almost always the dominant tradition (and in some periods the nearly exclusive one) was that of the Moderns, which constituted the French Rite in its (very) diverse states. That of the Ancients only appeared at the start of the nineteenth century, with the emergence of the Ancient and Accepted Scottish Rite. In the nineteenth and twentieth centuries, the only additions to these fundamental schemata were sometimes verbal developments, ever-longer speeches, and a few refinements in the ritual execution. These engendered textual expansion: a ritual of about a dozen pages in around 1750 is easily five times longer today. The twentieth century, particularly in France, also brought many innovations, in the form of both regrettable removals and additions that are sometimes hard to understand with regard to the original coherence of the systems.

It is also necessary to specifically mention the Scottish Rite of the eighteenth century (distinct from the Ancient and Accepted Scottish Rite), and more widely the high degrees. These have a more complex history, which we will examine later in this study.

III. MASONIC DISCOURSE ON RITUALS

As evoked in the chapter on symbols, the Masonic view of symbolism is somewhat ambiguous. Unsurprisingly, its discourse on rituals is not much more homogeneous. The justification for rituals and the importance accorded to them in Masonic life actually depend on the wider view taken of Freemasonry.

For "symbolist" or "traditional" Masons, and (clearly) for those who give a profound goal to their Masonry and readily make connections with the great spiritual or religious traditions of humanity, ritual, just like symbols, is an essential element. Moreover, it is primarily through ritual that members are molded, changed, and "born unto themselves." Here, ritual is therefore seen as the prime mover and key tool in the "initiatory quest." Evidently, it is not the goal, but the path that must be taken to reach it.

These "ritualist" Freemasons generally give great importance to the precise execution of written rituals, pay attention to the layout of the Lodge, and demand silence and dignity from the Officers taking part in a ceremony and all those attending. Everything must contribute to the feeling that an important action is taking place, and that in such a moment, Masonry is revealing one of its essential dimensions. At its extreme, ritual can become an end in itself: the slightest deviation is then considered a kind of blasphemy, or at least an extremely damaging fault, prompting anger and harsh comments. A sort of Masonic "bigotry" is not rare, and can take rather grotesque forms. The Freemasons themselves, who often have a highly developed sense of self-derision, often joke about this subject.

For those who hold this symbolist view, Masonic ritual does not so much claim to teach through discourse as to give the candidate an experience, in a sort of sacred drama or mystery (in the medieval sense of the term). This is intended to awaken spiritual echoes within him. Masons often assert that the true secret of Masonry lies not only in the "words, signs, and tokens" that are taught by the degrees and can be bought in all good bookshops, but in the personal experience of the beneficiary. Consequently, this secret is said to be incommunicable and inviolable. This view also makes it possible to justify the apparent absurdity of certain rituals, because it is not the literal meaning that matters, but the deep and existential meaning experienced within by the candidate.

The exact nature of this internal experience is nevertheless a matter of debate. It is possible to make a schematic distinction between the Guénonian view (which sees the initiation process as the transmission of a "spiritual influence" related to the "subtle composition" of the human being), and a more frequent and strongly psychological interpretation, comparing the Masonic ritual to psychoanalytical techniques, associations of ideas, the waking dream, or the psychodrama.

However, particularly in France, there is another category of Masons, often representing themselves as "humanist" or "secular" (or both), for whom Freemasonry above all has a philosophical and moral goal of social change. In this mindset, ritual appears less like the key element of Masonic action, because Masonry is supposed to act within the "profane world." Consequently, the Lodge is above all seen as a place for exchange, shared thought, and collective reaffirmation of the values to be protected: tolerance, equality, fraternity, human dignity, and often secularity. This immediately poses the question of how and whether ritual can be useful for such a project. However, once again, nothing is so black and white.

In fact, even Freemasons primarily interested in the "societal" aspects of Masonic work often welcome Masonic ritual with warmth and even interest, but its interpretation or justification is obviously different from that of the preceding discourse. In this case, the emphasis is on the pedagogical nature of the Masonic rites: the collective discipline for speaking, for example, which is precisely regulated in Lodges, and is supposed to teach respect for others and the need for thoughtful and considerate expression, because you only get one chance to speak. As concerns the ceremonies themselves, in allowing members to ascend through the degrees, it is emphasized that they are a sort of allegorical summary of the commitment, courage, and fidelity to one's principles that all Freemasons must show in their daily lives, outside of the Lodge itself: it is in a way a rather solemn representation of a work program.

Nevertheless, it is very often among this second category of Masons that the many complexities faced by candidates during Masonic initiation ceremonies have been judged somewhat arduous, unnecessarily complicated or rather incomprehensible, sometimes ridiculous, and even frankly obsolete. It was within this intellectual climate, which was largely predominant in France in the prewar period, that Masonic rituals were gradually "simplified" until they sometimes became nothing more than a rapid and vague opening protocol for the works of an assembly. As concerns the degrees themselves, often bestowed in meetings where numerous recipients are received at the same time, the "symbolic tests" were cut right back, with declarations of philosophical or political principles favored instead.

It is fair to say that nowadays, particularly since the end of the 1970s, such excesses are rarely seen. For all Obediences, with varying enthusiasm and goodwill, French Freemasons generally give a respectable place to the ritual dimension of their works. Some integrate primarily spiritualist and purely "initiatory" concerns without difficulty, while others do not give up on more societal interests.

With the diversity of rites (examined later on) and the various Masonic sensibilities, the everyday applications of the ritual framework of Freemasonry thus reveal considerable heterogeneity, or to put it more positively, an impressively rich variety. In any case, after almost three centuries of evolution, this dimension is, more than ever, an unavoidable part of the Masonic world, and one of its most irreducible components.

CHAPTER VIII
LEGENDS

As sufficiently established by research in cultural anthropology and by ethnographic data since the end of the nineteenth century, every ritual is more or less linked to a myth that provides its structure and meaning, even if the myth often appears second and not first. The same applies in Masonry, where the term "legends" is often preferred.

I. FROM THE MASONRY OF SYMBOLS TO THE MASONRY OF LEGENDS

History teaches us that Freemasonry was once restricted to very simple procedures, used just a few barely explained symbols, and had no recourse to legend. In any case, in its rituals, the text of the *Old Charges*, the origin and customs of which have already been mentioned, was essentially a dreamed (one might almost say "mythical") history evoking legendary monuments taken from the Bible, such as the Tower of Babel, or Solomon's Temple, without making them central concerns. Moreover, the text was read and not "played out."

In addition to this, the system in Scotland at the end of the seventeenth century, organized into two degrees, was above all based on two letters (J and B) and a few tools of the trade. A 1691 account from Scotland describes the transmission of the "Mason Word," which at the time was the principal component of a Masonic ceremony:

> It is like a Rabbinical tradition, taking the form of a commentary on Jachin and Boaz, the two pillars of Solomon's

Temple (1 Kings 7:21), with the addition of some secret sign given hand to hand, through which they recognize one another and become familiar with each other.

This was thus a descriptive, postural, and static Masonry, without any operative legend.

In the course of the eighteenth century, the symbolic apparatus of Freemasonry became organized, simplified, and diversified. Certain tools or objects were removed (particularly various types of stones), having become incomprehensible for purely Speculative Freemasons. Others symbols were added, sometimes based on translation errors. These symbols, borrowed from the building trade, as well as from mathematicians, had little if any remaining reference to their functional use. In the emblematic tradition of the sixteenth century, where they had already been widely used well before Freemasonry, they above all represented moral principles, such as rectitude, wisdom, and moderation. Moreover, symbols from alchemy, astrology, and even the Kabbalah gradually submerged the symbols, without completely replacing them, to form a much wider and more heterogeneous set.

This austere infrastructure was undoubtedly a little lacking in life. Nevertheless, a source containing all sorts of stories and fabulous characters which could be used to breathe life into the lodge was close at hand. The Bible had always been present in Lodges and, in these founding times, was part of all actions of social life, particularly in Protestant countries like Great Britain. In the 1720s, it was the Bible that would give the Masonic world its first legend. This would undeniably radically change the fate of Masonry.

II. HIRAM: THE FOUNDING LEGEND

The aim here is not to examine the numerous hypotheses which have been offered about the possible sources and circumstances behind the legend of Hiram. For our purposes, it is sufficient to note that it came into Masonic ritual between 1725 and 1730, with a new breadth to it. It was not simply a tale: it had become a "script." It no longer accompanied a ceremony, but structured it entirely.

Over time, this legend has also changed and developed in various ways. We will begin with a look at the key points.

It tells of Hiram, who is mentioned in the Bible, appearing either as a bronze worker (1 Kings), or an artisan with more varied skills (Book of Chronicles). However, these are passing mentions that go no further. The biblical text tells us absolutely nothing more about him.

In Masonic legend, Hiram becomes the architect of Solomon's Temple. Also governing all the workers (he is therefore the Master), he controls their progress through the "degrees" or "grades" of the profession. This legend presumes that there were three degrees at the time, which is refuted by all of medieval tradition. In order to become Masters and get the associated better salary, three "bad" Fellows ambush Hiram when he is alone on the site during a midday break, asking him for the secret word, which at a time when written documents were rarely used, allowed a person to be recognized and receive the correct pay for their skills. Faced with this felony, Hiram, a model of the upstanding worker, refuses. Mad with anger, the three fellows strike him a series of three blows, which kill him.

A few days later, his body is found under a mound of earth, hastily piled over him by his killers. Upon discovering his already rotting body, the Fellows sent by King Solomon express their horror using a word starting with the initials "M.B.," of which there are several variants. This came to replace the "Master's Word" known by Hiram. The Fellows do not know whether it has been possible to preserve this original word.

During the specific ceremony used in London from 1725, the Five Points of Fellowship known in Scotland since the seventeenth century became the way of elevating the candidate who replaces the dead Hiram. The latter is thus repeatedly replaced by all Masters admitted to this degree, who are told the "new Master's Word."

This necromantic ceremony contains numerous philosophical and religious echoes. The ritual clearly has a Christian foundation, explicitly exploited by the subsequent degrees, which for example play out Hiram's "resurrection." However, the value of this is mostly archetypal. Once this legend was introduced, Freemasonry took a new turn. Its "initiatory" dimension is highlighted by this "sacred drama" that is relived by the candidate, showing him the Masonic path to be like that of a symbolic death and rebirth. This is a classical theme, seen from the mysteries of antiquity to Saint Paul's evocation of the "old self" whom we must put off to access the Kingdom of God.

Of an entirely different nature to that of the first two degrees, the degree of Master begins a new series. It is the first level of—and the generating model for—the "high degrees," as they soon came to be called. Very quickly, further degrees appeared, extending and embellishing this legend, and adding others to it. By their very names, these degrees show their debt to the Hiramic degree: Perfect Master, Master Elect, Scottish Master, and so forth.

Little by little, once all of the themes associated with the death of Hiram had been exhausted (vengeance, burial, and replacement), the Bible provided other legendary themes, which in turn generated new degrees. We will return to this point later. The ceremonies of Freemasonry, with its many degrees, thus created a sort of "hierohistory," which is constantly and repeatedly played out. This initially very strong religious inspiration did die down, particularly in France and during the nineteenth century, while it remained basically intact in the Anglo-Saxon countries, Protestant lands with a strong biblical culture. In France, rituals were modified imperceptibly to replace an overly scriptural and religious vision with a more philosophical and "secular" perspective. Nevertheless, to this day, the basis in legend remains the most powerful source of Masonic rituals, and is the main attraction of the high degrees, where it flourishes and gives rise to much commentary.

III. HISTORY AND LEGEND: A MASONIC AMBIGUITY

The pervasiveness of legends in Masonic life, like the symbolic conventions on the topographical orientation of the Lodge (theoretically always east to west), or the timing of works (which always start at "midday" and supposedly end at "midnight"), is not without impact on how Freemasons see their origins and their history. The subject has given rise to so many misunderstandings that it is worth examining.

Through these artifices, Masonry recreates a codified world. This world provides a concrete, visual, and living support which brings a tangible and real-world element to an intellectual, moral, and spiritual process (in varying proportions) known to Freemasons as the "path of initiation." Legends and symbols give it its shape, decorations, and vocabulary. However, there is a risk of forgetting their conventional character and essentially heuristic nature: they are present not for themselves, but to allow or at least facilitate a certain mental journey. Experience nevertheless shows that many Freemasons do not actually see the difference between a legend (a tale which, like any myth, is timeless) and the chronicle of a history that leads from uncertain or distant origins to our time. This is what makes history a strange and often sensitive subject in the Masonic world.

A contemporary French Masonic scholar, Pierre Mollier, often jokes that "Freemasons love history...particularly sacred history!" This pleasantly ironic statement contains a great deal of truth, with significant consequences.

When Masonic legend began to form and then develop from at least the 1720s, there was also (as stated in the long historical preface of the 1723 *Constitutions*) an effort to write the great tale of the origins of Freemasonry. Obviously, modern historiographical criticism easily points out the errors, absurdities, and improbabilities of a narration that does not respect the rules or methods of documented history as we have conceived of it since the end of the nineteenth century. However, the legend of Hiram (the myth behind the degree of Master), which appeared at around the same time as the *Constitutions*, finds itself placed on the same level as the supposedly authentic chronicle of Freemasonry from its presumed origins in the Earthly Paradise!

This confusion of genres, which is evidently particularly severe in the points mentioned above, is nevertheless clear if extended to other domains. This is the case for the ongoing connection with the working Masons of the Middle Ages (which guaranteed the essentially modern institution of the Grand Lodge in 1717 a certain legitimacy), not to mention the links with Rosicrucianism (which itself is a literary fantasy) and with the Templars. For the latter, as we have seen, the illusion continues today in the minds of some of the public, as well as among Freemasons.

It seems likely that, to the great pleasure of Freemasons themselves, Masonic thought will continue these creative wanderings between real history and ritualized legend.

CHAPTER IX
DEGREES AND RITES

I. THE "BLUE" DEGREES: A PROGRESSIVE CREATION

The Masonry that emerges from the documentary void at the end of the seventeenth century in Scotland apparently had only two degrees: Apprentice and Fellow. In reality, from the outset, things were not so simple.

The first Scottish Masonic system was still really linked to the masonry craft; these links became highly tenuous in Scotland from the start of the eighteenth century, but only completely broke much later on. The precise names of the degrees were "Entered Apprentice" and "Fellowcraft or Master." This ambiguous terminology requires some unpicking.

Following the Schaw Statutes of 1598 and 1599, in Scotland there was an organizational duality that both opposed and brought together two structures: on the one hand the municipal guild and the bourgeois Masters (the Incorporation), who had a monopoly over employment and civil power, and on the other the Lodge itself, which controlled and guaranteed workers' ascent through the degrees of the profession. The Lodge would enter an apprentice who had been with his Master for several years. Prior to that point he was only registered by the Incorporation. Then, after a few years, he could become a Fellow of the Craft. Nevertheless, this was not an obligation, because the only real interest was that this reception allowed access to Master status, if necessary. This was not a degree, but a civil and professional status, given administratively by the Incorporation. Yet this Master status, which made a worker a boss, required significant financial expenditure, unless inherited from the father or obtained by marrying the daughter of another Master.

This was why the degree given by the Lodge was called "Fellow or Master." It was a Fellow degree (the last in the profession), which could allow access to the civil status of Master. Still, many workers never made this last step, and stayed "eternal apprentices."

When Freemasonry appeared in England, at the end of the seventeenth century and above all in the first two decades of the eighteenth century (by that time very detached from the Mason trade, but still recruiting widely among professionals, artisans, and shopkeepers), it still had just these two degrees, as shown by the 1723 *Constitutions*.

The third degree, that of Master—no longer a civil status but rather a real degree, conferred during a specific ritual ceremony—is first mentioned in London in 1725. It most likely existed before, but we do not know when it first emerged. We know the ritual thanks to Prichard's exposure in *Masonry Dissected*, published in 1730. This allows us to understand how it formed in relation to the preceding, two-degree system seen in Scottish rituals at the end of the seventeenth century: the salutation of the Fellowcraft degree (the Five Points of Fellowship) was transferred to this third, new degree, and was given a new explanation and justification through a link to a legend, namely that of Hiram. The former final degree of Fellowcraft became the second degree and was simultaneously almost entirely emptied of its content. Prichard's revelation shows that the only thing taught in it was the letter G (for *God* and *geometry*), revealed to the candidate in the "Middle Chamber." Once again, there is ambiguity here: according to whether we look at England or France, there were in fact two middle chambers.

The first, that of Prichard, still seen today in English Masonry, refers to a room elevated above the level of Solomon's Temple. This chamber is also mentioned in the biblical description. According to *Masonry Dissected*, it was in this chamber that Fellows received their "Wages" and were allowed to contemplate the letter G, which also denoted "Grandeur and Glory." However, when this system made it to the Continent, it mutated intriguingly.

The oldest description of the degree of Master in France is found in the 1744 revelation entitled *Le Catéchisme des francs-maçons* (*The Catechism of the Freemasons*). In it, we can see that the Middle Chamber has moved to the third degree. The Five Points of Fellowship have, rather logically, become the "Five Perfect Points of Mastership." But where was this new Middle Chamber? Apparently, in the middle of the Temple, that is a priori in the sanctuary (the Hekal). Gradually, the rituals for the degree of Master in France did bring about the appearance of a space temporarily hidden by a curtain in the east of the Master's Lodge. This was the Debir, the Holy of Holies, the most sacred place in this Temple, where God resided in the darkness. This takes us from an elevated Middle Chamber to a Middle Chamber in horizontal terms, between the Ulam (the Lodge forecourt, itself now assimilated with Solomon's Temple) and the Debir. This little-known topographical difference between French (or continental) Masonry and English Masonry still exists to this day. Is it the result of a translation error, like certain Masonic symbols, or of a deliberate development? Even today nobody can say.

But why are these three degrees described as "blue?" In June 1727, the register of records of the first Grand Lodge of London mentions for the first time the fact that the Venerable Master and the Wardens of Lodges should wear "the jewels of Masonry on a white ribbon." In March 1731, a further ruling from the Grand Lodge states that "the Grand Master, his Deputy, and his (Grand) Wardens will wear gold or silver-gilt jewels on blue ribbons around their necks, and their leather aprons will be trimmed with blue silk."

However, in the same period, it was the British who introduced Masonry to France, imposing their customs. Yet a printed disclosure published in 1744, *Le Secret des francs-maçons* (*The Secret of the Freemasons*), states that "in these assemblies, each Brother has an apron made of a white hide, and the cords must also be made of hide. Some wear them as they are, with no decoration, while others trim them with a blue ribbon." Further on, the same author tells us that "the Worshipful Master, the two Wardens, the Secretary, and the Treasurer" wear "a blue cord shaped into a triangle." Thus, it is clear that at some point between around 1730 and around 1745, in both France and England but based on an English initiative, the aprons of particular Lodge members became blue, whereas this had formerly been just for Grand Officers. In fact, there were originally two shades of blue: light and dark. These two shades were successively adopted by the Order of the Garter, the highest distinction of the British monarchy. The light blue remained in "Blue" Lodges, and the dark blue, simply called "Garter Blue" in England, was that of the Grand Lodge. Coincidentally, light blue was also the color of France's Order of the Holy Spirit, the highest award under the French monarchy.

In general, this teaches us that from the beginnings of Freemasonry, Masonic decorations were given a color deliberately evoking one of the country's highest distinctions. Freemasonry, gradually recruiting from all social classes, quickly came to consider itself a new aristocracy. From 1744, it was said in France that the Lodges "don't look at class, because every Brother is reputed to be a gentleman."

II. "SUBLIME DEGREES" AND SIDE DEGREES

Nobody really knows why or how there was a desire to go beyond the first three degrees and create, then spread, new degrees above them, called the "high degrees" or, more often from the eighteenth-century in

France, the "sublime degrees of Masonry." In England, they are often called "side degrees." In modern-day France, the terms "perfect degrees" and "wise degrees" are also used.

In fact, it all began with the degree of Master, which in terms of its structure, as described above, was the first of the high degrees (and not the last of the blue degrees). However, from the 1730s, and above all from 1740, particularly in France, but also in Great Britain, many degrees appeared, provoking passionate reactions from Brothers. Throughout the whole (or almost the whole) eighteenth century, these were the degrees that were most highly esteemed in Masonic circles. It was thought that the blue degrees were just introductory, and that "serious matters" in Masonry began with the high degrees. A model had been created: that of the degree based on a legend, with the candidate required to partially reenact a (generally) biblical story. This new line would be constantly pursued.

The first high degrees drew upon the events following the death of Hiram: his vengeance (the different elect degrees), his burial (Irish Master, unexpectedly borrowing from the tales told by the Jesuits of Chinese ceremonies paying homage to the dead), and his replacement at the head of the workers (Scottish Master of the 3 JJJ in Paris).

Once the possible developments related to the first Temple (that of Solomon) were exhausted, the Masons moved on to the Second Temple (that of Zerubbabel), reconstructed after the liberation of the Jews in Babylon by an order from Cyrus. Between approximately 1740 and 1760, the degree of Knight of the East and of the Sword was thus the most widespread final degree, at the top of the Masonic structure. It played out the evocation found in the Book of Nehemiah (4:12) of the struggles suffered by the Jews returning to Jerusalem, who while building "worked with one hand and held their weapons with the other." It should be noted in passing that this image already featured in Ramsay's famous *Discourse* of 1736, but was applied to the Crusaders fighting the infidels to take back the Holy Land. Although it is very improbable that Ramsay himself (as some have believed) contributed to its creation, there is no doubt that the theme for this degree was taken from this text, which would soon become very famous. By the same token, the extremely general motif of chivalry entered the Masonic corpus. A whole new world opened up.

As already mentioned, Masonic chivalry rapidly identified itself with the Templar legend. From the Rite of Strict Observance to the degree of Knight Kadosh (which was highly controversial from the eighteenth century because of its sometimes vengeful tone, which became caricatural towards the end of the nineteenth century), the introduction of this legend, with all its variants and refinements, also put the idea of a possible connection (obviously an illusion) between the martyred order and Freemasonry itself into the collective consciousness of Masons. As the twentieth century approached, the rituals of this degree sometimes glorified the "heroic" combat of the cursed "throne and altar" knights. From this, we can see how far Freemasonry had changed since the first Masonic mention of knights who, in the Holy Land, died to defend the Christian faith and the Latin kingdoms of Palestine. In passing, we can also see how the same legendary, symbolic, and ritual theme, in this changing and flexible world of Freemasonry, can serve extremely different ends.

Without claiming to be exhaustive, it is necessary to give a separate place in the inextricable jungle of the high degrees to those attached to the *Écossais de la Voûte* ("Scots of the Vault"). This fundamental Masonic legend reveals that the Master's Word (the previous one, changed out of precaution and necessity after Hiram's tragic death) was hidden in the crypt of Solomon's Temple. Kept safe over the ages by a caste of initiates, and then forgotten, this crypt and the word hidden there are rediscovered by the candidate. The word in question, of which there are many forms, is nothing other than a variant of God's name in Hebrew tradition, sometimes called the "unspeakable word" in Masonic rituals: this is the secret, the final key to the traditional Masonic edifice.

This legend is often associated with that of the "Royal Arch," for which the primary source is a tale dating back to the start of the fifth century and attributed to Philostorgius, who tells of the chance discovery of a vault during the reconstruction of the Temple. This theme is at the heart of the British Royal Arch degree, considered in Britain to be an indispensable complement to a degree, and not as a true high degree. In fact, the British Royal Arch degree also incorporates a part of the degree of the Knight of the Orient and that of the *Écossais de la Voûte*: a real concentration of the major legends of Masonic tradition.

Finally, Freemasonry, born in a Christian culture, has given a major place to the central figure of this religion: Jesus Christ. This is visible in the degree of Rose-Croix (Knight or Sovereign Prince), which appeared at the start of the 1760s in eastern France. Centered on the discovery of the three theological virtues (faith, hope, and love) and the contemplation of the calvary scene, the name of the degree links it to the Rosicrucian fantasy, which had a big impact in the seventeenth century, first in Germany, then in France and Great Britain, but without any real line of descent. The "true word" that is revealed here is no longer just one of God's names, but that of the human God according to the Gospel of Matthew (1:23): Emmanuel. During the last third of the eighteenth century, this degree was considered the *nec plus ultra* of Masonry: there was nothing beyond it. It incorporated a Protestant-type Last Supper, with a ritual ending in the words taken from the Gospel: "It is finished."

III. FROM DEGREES TO RITES

There were already dozens of high degrees, with decorations of aprons, cords, and ribbons (which had changed from blue to black, red, green, or white), by the mid-eighteenth century, and well over a hundred before the French Revolution.

We rarely know the authors of these rituals, but some of the social circles in which they emerged, as well as the intellectual sensibilities that favored them, can be identified. They still spread randomly, through chance meetings, and often by correspondence, because there was great exchange between Freemasons across the whole of Europe, where the default language in cultivated circles was French. Gradually, from the 1750s, and even more so in the following decade, two movements emerged: the first aimed to give a certain order to degrees and to establish a given process for attributing them, while the other aimed to control practice and transmission. On the one hand, there was Masonic science, and on the other, power. To this day, the constant conflict between these two views continues.

The sequence of these degrees only became established very gradually, with many variations in detail, but at the turn of the 1760s there were already a few well-established landmarks. The first was the "Hiramic" sequence (Master Elect, Perfect Master, Irish Master, Scottish Master). There were also the *Écossais de la Voûte* and the Royal Arch, as well as Masonic chivalry with its prototype, the Knight of the East, and, much later, the Kadosh and finally the Rose-Croix, long judged to be unsurpassable. Moreover, certain degrees held out in the competition for this status of *nec plus ultra*, including the somewhat Hermetic-inspired degree of Knight of the Sun.

This was when the notion of rite (or *Rit*, as it was still written in France at the start of the nineteenth century) emerged. This word, which today dominates everyday Masonic vocabulary, particularly in France (it is hardly used in England), actually has two very distinct meanings.

The first and oldest meaning refers to the particular order in which degrees are attributed, with some retained and others left aside, in a supposedly coherent system. Thus, in the mid-1780s, the Grand Orient de France, or more precisely, its General Grand Chapter, established four "orders" (a fifth, meant to bring together all the other Masonic degrees of all systems, would be added). These were four identifiable high degrees (Elect, Scottish, Knight of the East, Rose-Croix), which formed what would later be called the French Rite.

A few years earlier, between Lyon and Strasbourg and on German foundations, (the Strict Templar Observance mentioned above), the Rectified Scottish Rite (or Regime) had been structured into four Masonic degrees (the fourth was Scottish Master of Saint Andrew), and two classes of the inner order: an order of chivalry culminating with the Beneficent Knight of the Holy City. Based on degrees of alchemical inspiration, a Philosophical Scottish Rite also formed. After the French Revolution, under the Empire and the July Monarchy, the Rite of Misraïm then that of Memphis appeared, in ninety and ninety-five degrees, claiming to be inspired by the mysteries of Egypt.

Finally, in 1804, coming from America, the Ancient and Accepted Scottish Rite imported its thirty-three degrees to France. These were governed by a Supreme Council, and the highest degree was Sovereign Grand Inspector General. This rite was to have a great future in France, becoming a leading jurisdiction of high degrees.

These degrees numbered from just a few to several dozen depending on the rites, with the great classics reappearing everywhere. Looking at the list, these were often the only degrees really bestowed: it quickly became common not to use a real ceremony for all of them, and to transmit them virtually instead, by "communication." This involved just the signing of a document. Many of these degrees were never even written down, particularly those of the Egyptian Rites. Others were secondary degrees, and were sometimes studied, but never or very rarely put into practice. Essentially the key degrees in Masonic ritual were and still are those cited above.

However, during the nineteenth century, the word *rite* took on a second meaning. This time, it came to designate the particular formula for the rituals of the first three degrees, and the detail of their ceremonies. In the eighteenth century, except for local variants, all the Lodges, whatever high-degree rites they practiced, used basically the same ritual. This would later be called the French Rite, emerging out of the oldest heritage in French Masonry, which came over from England at the start of the 1720s. In the second half of the nineteenth century, Blue or "Scottish" Lodges also appeared. For the blue degrees, they actually practiced a variant of the French Rite. This situation changed from the first quarter of the nineteenth century.

With the early rupture between the Supreme Council of France and the Grand Orient in 1804, the members of the Ancient and Accepted Scottish Rite resolved to give their Blue Lodges a specific ritual. This is represented in the *Guide des maçons écossais* (*Guide for Scottish Masons*), which is greatly inspired by an English disclosure of 1760, *The Three Distinct Knocks*. It shares particularities of the "Scottish" Lodges seen in France in the eighteenth century. From then on, a distinction was made between the (Blue) Lodges of the Scottish Rite and those of the French Rite. Later, at the start of the twentieth century, the Rectified Scottish Rite had returned to France after several decades of absence, and a few Blue Lodges also began practicing its ritual, which was very different from that of the first two rites. Finally, we should not forget the continuing presence of Blue Lodges of the Egyptian Rite, whose ritual only acquired very specific characteristics late on, during the 1960s.

Such was the ritual landscape of Symbolic Lodges (another name for Blue Lodges in France). A Brother or Sister in France might be asked the rite of their Lodge. In England, this question would have been illogical: the same ritual was practiced everywhere, and had no name, but concerned the Masonry of the first three degrees, which were always called the "Craft." There were only very slight differences between Lodges in England, defining what were known as the "Workings," the most famous of which have names, for example, the "Emulation Working." Nevertheless, when this ritual was introduced in France, then translated into French in the mid-1920s, it was given the name *Rite Émulation*.

In the contemporary period, the creation of rites continued. At the start of the 1970s, an Operative Rite of Solomon was developed in Paris, skillfully combining elements borrowed from the French Rite, the Rectified Scottish Rite, and the Emulation "Rite."

IV. MASONIC PROGRESSION: VANITY, OR A "SERIOUS GAME?"

Just like symbols and rituals, the Masonic degrees have always been a target of mockery by the "profane," who ask: "Why do they need such vain and pompous titles?" Or: "What are the Masons hiding behind by following the strange meanderings of these often so disconcerting scales of degrees?" The criticism is nothing new, but the attitude of Masons themselves towards the high degrees has also always been nuanced, or at least very varied.

There is no doubt that the success of Freemasonry, from its origins to the end of the nineteenth century, particularly in France, has been greatly linked to the unfailing vogue for the high degrees. For Ancien Régime France, it is understandable that prosperous bourgeois citizens, then later simple shopkeepers, found it flattering (although completely illusory) to become a "Knight" or a "Sovereign Prince." Let us not forget that common assertion in Masonic texts of the time: the Lodge proclaims high equality, so all Brothers are considered to be "gentlemen." The most eloquent sign (which means little to us today) was that everyone wore the sword in Lodges: at the time, in the outside world, only nobles and soldiers had this right, and they guarded it fiercely.

Nevertheless, we should not be fooled about the extent of this supposed equality. Social divides remained, and the Lodges chose their members, basically reproducing the divisions of the profane world. In bourgeois Lodges, the "Servant Brothers" (domestics serving at the Masonic banquet) could only very rarely become Apprentices. In the army, where Freemasonry prospered, most regiments took part in Masonry, but they usually had two Lodges: one for the high-born officers and the other for the commoners—the "lowly officers"—of the ranks.

However, this explanation seems a little simplistic today, and this all-too-human vanity has limited meaning in our democratic societies, where it seems to have little influence. In order to understand the ongoing attraction to the high degrees among Freemasons, we must therefore find a motive that has remained a constant from the eighteenth century to the present day.

The only explanation seems to be a certain fascination with (or at least a very keen interest in) mystery and a strange experience that resembles both Italian comedy and the psychodrama: the ritual ceremony in which the applicant, for several minutes, successively incarnates biblical or mythical figures. The high degrees are both disturbing and attractive for many perfectly healthy-minded Freemasons, who are normally cultivated and good companions, because of the extraordinary variety of subjects, extreme situations, and philosophical or legendary themes that structure them. These provoke surprise, reflection, doubt, and confusion. Now, in our "disenchanted" world, this "serious game" or "Grand Game" is a completely exotic psychological and intellectual experience.

Obviously, some individuals get it wrong: the search for mysterious knowledge, and in some cases psychic, magnetic, or other powers, is part of the folklore of a certain caricatured Masonry, but some members take it seriously. Moreover, even for those not guilty of this confusion (which is essentially the basis for all kinds of sects), the mystery surrounding Freemasonry still has its collective effect. The precision with which certain Masons, despite not adhering to any dubious mysticism, carry out Masonic ritual and even the Masonic "bigotry" evoked above suggests that for its members, especially in a secularized country such as France, Masonry sometimes plays the ambiguous role of a sort of substitute of religion, mostly without their realizing it. The high degrees are the willing and luxurious sanctuaries of this.

Undoubtedly, many "secular" Masons would reject this approach, but for an outside observer, the denial is not necessarily convincing. Although many of them are in favor of the "simplification" of rituals, there are also many who are uncompromising about the position of a candlestick or the precise clothing of a long-desired degree.

Despite this, since the end of the nineteenth century, particularly in France, there has been a movement in Freemasonry that is more or less hostile to the existence of "high degrees." Born in both the French Rite and the Scottish Rite, this movement denounces their outdated pomp and above all, the aristocratic or even autocratic (or in any case nondemocratic) methods of those who manage them, particularly the Supreme Council of the Ancient and Accepted Scottish Rite. In a Masonry that at the time was primarily engaged in the political struggle, this attitude was logical, and the argument held strong. Today, this vision is declining in most French Masonic circles because of structural reform, but there is still sometimes a certain reserve with regard to the high degrees, on very different bases.

Certain Freemasons, fascinated by the "operative origins" and particularly by the Compagnonnage (which, as we have said, is not actually the direct source of Speculative Freemasonry, but has given it many of its customs), consider that "true" Masonry lies only within the first three degrees: those most directly linked to the evocation of the craft of masons. This element is almost entirely absent in the high degrees, many of which are Masonic only in name. From this viewpoint, the ideal Masonic career therefore consists in reproducing, "in spirit," that of a simple cathedral builder: "really becoming a Master" is thus a life's work. This is a respectable view, not without obvious sobriety and real demands, but it is clearly a minority position in Freemasonry today.

CHAPTER X
THE ORDER AND THE OBEDIENCES

I. FROM THE LODGE TO THE GRAND LODGES

When the first Grand Lodge of London was founded in June 1717, it is almost certain that those assembled did not realize they had created an institution. At the very most, they thought it was an annual meeting to pool the forces of a few weak Lodges that were seeking wealthy protectors. However, they had just laid the foundations for a model which in the space of just a few years would be applied throughout the Masonic world.

Obviously, there were Lodges before the Grand Lodges, and the Grand Lodge of London and Westminster moreover took many years to convince English Masons of the need to join forces and to pay the newly created fees to maintain the structure. At the turn of the 1720s, however, the die was cast: the Grand Lodges would govern and influence the fate of Freemasonry. The 1723 *Constitutions* were the first, most striking, most innovative, and longest-lasting manifestation of this. They established a single text for the only historical account that was now acceptable, showing (against all evidence) that the Grand Lodge had always existed. It also defined the only allowable rules of operation for the Lodges. From then on, there was constant debate in Masonic circles: Had Freemasonry lost in depth what it had gained in power and influence? In other words, were the Grand Lodges (the word "Obediences" is more generally used, as not all of them bore the name "Grand Lodge") a wonderful innovation or a necessary evil?

Once again, the cultural difference between the British founders and the French emulators quickly became clear. To this day, the Grand Lodge in England has been integrated into the establishment. In a country where there was a revolution to definitively restore the monarchy (although in parliamentary form), the Grand Master, like the king or queen, stays in place for decades, and receives homages and marks of respect, but has almost no power. Nevertheless, all English Freemasons revere the apparatus and complex hierarchy of the Grand Lodge, as is the case for the most ancient institutions of the kingdom: only the Grand Lodge can provide Masonic salvation! In contrast, in France, the first Grand Masters were only those "of the regular Lodges of the Kingdom." For a long time, the "Grand Lodge" itself was nothing more than an embryonic and little-esteemed administration, particularly in provinces that, under the Ancien Régime, were still hostile to the Parisian authorities. The contemporary situation inherited these contradictions.

Federations of Lodges with varying juridical and organizational methods, Obediences became associations governed by the 1901 law on associations (for which many Freemason parliamentarians voted). They gave Masonry a moral character, but also administrative and management tools. Moreover, they are the visible face of Freemasonry, particularly for the media. The position of Freemasons themselves regarding these official showcases is ambiguous.

On the one hand, Freemasons willingly develop a feeling of affiliation, which leads them to see "their" Obedience in the best light, to take pride in their membership, and to take part (with varying degrees of malice) in the small disputes between Obediences that pepper Masonic life. The extreme division of the Masonic landscape, specific to France, often leads to stereotyping regarding the identities of Obediences. The press kits regularly used by newspapers only propagate these rather caricatured views: for example, the Grand Orient is said to be "left wing," while the

Grand Lodge is described as "symbolist," and another Obedience might be characterized as "highly Christian." These convenient labels are of limited value. While not entirely untrue, they give the public a greatly oversimplified image of a far more nuanced and complex internal reality. There are many divisions within Obediences and even within Lodges, and a Grand Lodge cannot be compared to a political or religious movement whose activists share a single faith, unless we take a party with countless currents as our point of comparison.

Moreover—and this is the second aspect—many Freemasons also, in principle, maintain a degree of reserve with regard to their Obedience, its apparatus, its formalities, and its procedures. This distrust is even more pronounced in regional Lodges, where the "Parisian authorities" are willingly mocked.

In fact, an Obedience must respect a Constitution or general regulation, and issue warnings, particularly for late payment of contributions (called "capitations" in the French Masonic world). It must manage disagreements between members, or between Lodges themselves (there is thus a "Masonic legal system") and regularly issue sanctions (suspensions, removals, and so forth.): the French mindset, always quick to criticize power, has ample material here to exercise its wit on the Masonic administration.

Nevertheless, Obediences are the interface between two levels of the Masonic phenomenon: that of the Brothers and Sisters, and that of the other Grand Lodges of Freemasons abroad.

II. THE MASONIC INSTITUTIONS: ADMINISTRATION AND DIPLOMACY

The disputes sometimes seen in the Masonic world are clearly, in part, those of the men and women who populate it. However, they are much more often those of Obediences, with their eternal claims of precedence, age, and authenticity.

97

In Great Britain and the American states, where there is generally only one Grand Lodge, being a Freemason and belonging to *the* Grand Lodge are one and the same. In a country like France, where there are a dozen well-known and stable Obediences today, along with half a dozen more modest (or even marginal) ones, and a few dozen poorly identified structures of debatable Masonic nature, the question is entirely different. The problem of "inter-Obedience relations" is one of the most frequent issues faced by the Grand Masters of various Obediences. They fight for the supposed influence that the "Masonic Order" might have over society in general, and about the desire to impose a particular vision of Freemasonry and its driving principles. Nevertheless, the sometimes very strong ego of certain dignitaries and their entourages does not help.

The Masonic hierarchy, which is essentially elective, has also led to branches of participation in power, which readily borrow methods from the "profane world." Competition is fierce, and the methods used are sometimes hardly respectable. Moreover, and importantly, a person is simply "president" of an association, but in Masonry, they are a "Grand Master," a "Sovereign Grand Commander," or even a "Grand Prior." The exaggerated titles, justified by a long past that explains their origin and initial meaning, sometimes give men and women who have lived a decent but sometimes rather obscure social life a feeling of real recognition, which can be rather disturbing and make them lose their sense of reality. Once again, the "normal" Masons often watch the resulting "leaders' battle" with some concern.

At the international level, the same spirit of competition prevails between the Grand Lodges. Since at least 1929, the Masonic world has been officially split into two sides. There is the side of "regularity," based in London with the United Grand Lodge of England, which describes itself as the "Mother Grand Lodge of the World." Many

Obediences around the world recognize this primacy, and "regular" Masonry is still very dominant worldwide. Among the principles that it imposes on the Grand Lodge that it "recognizes" in each country are the belief in a Supreme Being, the ban on any political discussion within the Lodge, and the exclusion of women. Naturally, the regular Grand Lodges have no official relationship with those that are not (at least officially) regular.

The other group is that of the "irregular" Obediences, which obviously object to this unflattering description. This is the sensibility that is predominant in France and in a few countries influenced by France in the Masonic domain, such as Belgium or Italy. Nevertheless, it should not be assumed that this second group is homogeneous, or that it is the polar opposite of Anglo-Saxon regularity in all domains. It is true that in France, under the leadership of the Grand Orient, we readily speak of "liberal and nondogmatic Freemasonry," but there are also Obediences which, although they are not recognized by London, perfectly or mostly respect the principles of regularity.

III. A "FREE MASON" IN A "FREE LODGE?"

In 1956, the experienced and knowledgeable Freemason Marius Lepage (1902–1972) published the first of many editions of *L'Ordre et les Obédiences* (*The Order and the Obediences.*) In this book, he compared these two notions and developed the idea that:

> Although the Order is universal, the different Obediences are particularist, influenced by the social, religious, economic, and political conditions of the countries in which they develop.
>
> The Order is essentially undefinable and absolute; the Obediences are subject to all the fluctuations inherent in the congenital weakness of the human mind.

The reason for the book's success was that many Masons recognized themselves in Marius Lepage's statements, without giving up on the existence of Obediences (the few attempts to do so never really prospered).

Thus, for all within this undefinable "Order," there remained a common denominator: the Lodge. Here, we are on even more consensual ground within Masonic thought: the Freemason only really exists in his Lodge. The rest is of little consequence. Oswald Wirth, Lepage's Master and himself a very famous Masonic author whose works are still read today, spread the popular phrase: "A Free Mason in a Free Lodge." However this is understood (and much comment is possible), it highlights an essential dimension of the Masonic project, which we will examine later: even before "freedom of thought" (an expression with strong philosophical connotations, which can be used in many ways and is not unanimously accepted), Freemasons emphasize freedom of the mind. Many of them even consider it to be the key value, which they would undoubtedly be least willing to abandon. Thus, the Lodge is basically an antisect.

PART THREE

THE ETHICS AND SPIRITUALITY OF FREEMASONRY

CHAPTER XI
FREEMASONRY AND RELIGION

I. A FOUNDING AMBIGUITY

It would be pointless to deny that Freemasonry was born in a religious context. England and Scotland in the seventeenth and eighteenth centuries were Protestant countries, imbibed with biblical culture, and to this day, religious affiliation is a component of social identity. Naturally, this religious origin can be seen in the symbols and rituals, as well as in the first rules and the oldest customs of Freemasonry.

Clearly, it is not insignificant that the Lodge was identified with Solomon's Temple, that the Master embodied Hiram (traditionally represented by a figurative exegesis like a kind of Jesus Christ), and that the high degrees looked for a word which is most often just one of the variants of God's name in the Bible. Since the origins of Freemasonry, the Bible has been omnipresent in the Lodge. All the vows are sworn on this holy book of the Protestant world, and as Masonry developed, it drew the legends for all its degrees from it. From the eighteenth century, in both France and England, every lodge had a chaplain, generally chosen from the ministers of an established religion, because every Lodge meeting began and ended with prayers.

The famous first of the "General Heads" of Anderson's 1723 *Constitutions*, "Concerning God and Religion," which stipulates that a Mason "will never be a stupid Atheist nor an irreligious Libertine," attracted much comment, particularly in France,[16] but the term "Denominations," used later in the work, explicitly refers to the different Christian churches. Could an official text, destined for publication, written by a pastor (James Anderson) under the supervision of a minister of the Church of England (John Theophilus Desaguliers), have attempted to say anything else?

The oldest concerns of these Lodges were neither philosophical, nor symbolic, nor "initiatory." They were above all moral and charitable.

Inspired by the spirit of brotherhoods, which had spread throughout Europe from around the eleventh century, the first lodges primarily aimed to manage the Common Box for helping those hit by illness or accident. This was a typically religious task in Christian Europe, generally carried out by the Church or the brotherhoods that basically depended on it, and which, like Lodges, already had banners, decorations, communal banquets, and certain rituals.

However, things were never this simple. British Freemasonry has always banned religious discussions and insisted on the fact that it is neither a religion nor a substitute for religion. Although Freemasonry was the center of what was called "liberty of conscience" in eighteenth-century England, in the Anglo-Saxon context, this possibly misleading expression simply meant "religious freedom."

In a country which had been through a century and a half of bloody wars between different religions, Freemasonry (like the Royal Society from 1660) imposed the most absolute religious tolerance in its rules and customs, except for outright atheism. This was a novelty, and was almost

---

16   And perhaps even far too much: a text can always be removed from its context and made to say almost anything, but for a person who reads this text in light of the political and religious climate in England at the start of the eighteenth century, its meaning is very clear, and in this founding time, it was never disputed: Freemasons had to be members of a religion of some form.

unique in Europe. It was a sort of mini revolution, with Freemasonry acting as both a product and a player.

In Great Britain (and later in America), where religion and state have been cohabiting for over three centuries, this is still the case, and nobody bats an eyelid. The same cannot be said for France.

II. A CONTRASTING HISTORY

A priori, Freemasonry stood little chance of prospering in France: it was moving from a Protestant country of religious tolerance and parliamentarianism to a Catholic kingdom in a regime of revocation (since 1685, Protestants were denied full existence) and the king, or his main minister (Cardinal Fleury) were all-powerful. However, against all expectations, Lodges spread quickly in France. Still, Freemasonry in the country acquired new characteristics.

In the Enlightenment, Freemasonry never became a hotbed of anti-religious activism. On the contrary, it was forced to make deals with the authorities and offer guarantees to the Church. This did not stop it being condemned by the pope from 1738, and again in 1751. Thanks to the passive complicity of Parliament, it is true that the bull was never recorded and remained without legal effect, but from this time, there was a fracture between Freemasonry and the Vatican.

Under the Empire, a fairly Voltairian bourgeoisie came to power. It often contained high numbers of Masons, because it brought together the elite of the regime. However, during the nineteenth century, everywhere in Europe the Catholic Church was pitted against the rise of nonbelief and explicitly condemned everything that was not in allegiance with it: Freemasonry was stigmatized again. Yet in France in the second half of the nineteenth century, as we will see, there was also a political evolution.

The repression of all free political expression had almost automatically thrown the liberal circles towards the Lodges, which were more difficult to monitor. This social and political change in the mentality of Lodges was accompanied by increasing hostility to *the* religion: that which for over a century and a half had always fought against Freemasonry, and which from the end of the eighteenth century had accused it of political and religious conspiracy. This is particularly seen in Abbé Barruel's highly inventive *Mémoires pour servir à l'histoire du jacobinisme* (*Memoirs Illustrating the History of Jacobinism*, 1798–1805).

Thus, only in France and the Catholic countries that underwent similar political evolution (such as Belgium and Italy) did Freemasonry move from liberty of conscience (religion) to liberty of thought: a euphemism designating sworn opposition to churches in general.

Over the course of around fifty years, all parties played a part: the Church by showering Freemasonry with increasingly violent and even insulting condemnations, and Freemasonry by continuing its path towards systematic anticlericalism. This movement was, rather logically, accompanied by the appearance of "atypical Republicans," particularly around Charles Renouvier and later Ferdinand Buisson, who wanted to launch a secular morality, or even a "secular religion." Nevertheless, nobody was surprised when, in 1877, the Grand Orient removed the obligation (which had only been official since 1849) for its members to believe in God and the immortal soul. Only the English Freemasons (who could not understand such a situation, having forgotten Catholic domination centuries ago) were angered and decided to definitively break off the already very fragile connections with the French Masons.

The 1905 law on the separation of churches and state, written and voted upon by a political personnel containing many Freemasons, was the symbol and the peak of this ideological war. It also established the now classical portrait of the radical-socialist Freemason, a freethinker and a "cleric eater," a French specialty beloved by the satirical newspapers and magazines of the Far Right, against a background of anti-Semitism: the "Judeo-Masonic conspiracy."

In a disenchanted twenty-first century, and in a highly secular France where Catholicism is severely weakened (or at least deprived of most of its former power), such tensions would be meaningless. Consequently, they have eased since the 1970s. The most advanced Catholics realized that Freemasons were not nihilists, and certain Freemasons returned to their ceremonies and symbols.

Forgetting religion and its secular disputes, the Lodges began speaking of spirituality.

III. A "SECULAR SPIRITUALITY?"

Indisputably, there are still many Freemasons, or even whole Lodges or Obediences in France, for whom religious issues are extremely sensitive. They see any statement in favor of an even slightly religious vision as a serious infraction of the "secular cause." These positions are even sometimes expressed with a certain virulence. This is still part of the culture, and sometimes, when taken to their extreme, these attitudes contribute to a certain French Masonic folklore. However, it is clear that another approach is becoming increasingly common. Strangely, on many points, it overlaps with the approaches of Masonries—primarily Anglo-Saxon ones, though this is also present in France—for whom the reference to a transcendence and explicitly to God or even Christ is important. This gives rise to an unusual restructuring of Masonic thought on these issues.

For several years, Lodges have favored the expression "secular spirituality," which attempts to describe this new perspective. The expression is deliberately ambiguous, because of the polysemy of the adjective *secular*.

However, as is typical of Masonry, this lack of precision allows many to identify with the expression.

For some, it simply means that being "secular" (understood as completely detached from any religious consideration) does not stop a person asking the fundamental questions of existence: the whole history of philosophy proves this! Just a few years ago, a Grand Master therefore explained to the convent of the Grand Orient de France (who did not boo or jeer) that "secularity [was] not an excuse for ignorance."

Nevertheless, this also subtly means that the goal of Masonic work has discreetly refocused on human destiny, the meaning of life, and even the ultimate purpose. This is a first aspect of the phenomenon. In other cases, but in the same spirit, there is a tendency to confuse spirituality with secular morality, which is clearly more reductive. Once again, however, on questions of bioethics, for example, we are redirected to the sources of morality (in the almost Bergsonian sense of this question: What is the specific norm of a "secular" morality, compared to another, religious-based, morality?). In all cases, we can see how far things have changed since the concerns seen almost a century ago.

For others, it is the word *spirituality* that is emphasized. One Grand Master of a major French Obedience stated that "spirituality is a genus, whereas religion is a species." From this, we are to understand that Free-masonry is higher, broader, and more all-embracing.

It is by advancing in the universe, which may be codified without his knowing it, that man can be united with the Great Whole and see meaning, without necessarily needing to refer to a god like the one seen in traditional religions. This "holistic" view, a confused version of which is found in the errancy of the New Age, and traces of which are also seen in Lodges, attempts to reconcile scientific data and the aspirations of a quest for meaning. Here, symbolism becomes the privileged tool in a reflection that juggles concepts and combines ideas. This second, highly valued, approach to "secular" spirituality is undoubtedly the center of gravity of contemporary French Masonic thought.

Finally, those who hold a more traditionally religious view willingly rally behind the expression, giving it another, more concrete interpretation: any individual who is not engaged in the ministry of any church is "secular." This therefore includes most believers and the faithful. In this perspective, secular spirituality is not opposed to religious faith, but can even be an extension of it. Therefore Masonic practice does not contradict or duplicate religious practice. It allows it to find new fields of activity and inquiry, in a symbolic and ritual context that has (as we have seen) extremely religious origins.

One high dignitary of the United Grand Lodge of England, reputed to be the world center of "believer" Masonry, stated at the end of 2011 that Freemasonry had nothing to do with spirituality, and that this was precisely what religion was for. He said that the role of Freemasonry was only to create men of high morality. These words are undoubtedly disconcerting for many French Freemasons, highly attached to the secular cause and used to a much more schematic view of English Freemasonry. This is further proof, if it is really required, that the relationship between Freemasonry (in all its components) and spirituality is even more complex than we (and sometimes Freemasons themselves) tend to think.

CHAPTER XII
FREEMASONRY AND SOCIETY

Since its early development, Speculative Freemasonry has had an ambiguous relationship (to say the least) with civil society, or the "profane world" as Masons call it.

Although Masonry in England has always been concerned to preserve its "initiatory" image, banning any incursion into the political domain, the first Grand Masters nevertheless had ulterior political motives, and constantly sought the protection of authority, placing the social elite of the country in prestigious positions in its hierarchy. When Masonry came to France, the first text that it produced there, Ramsay's famous *Discourse*, already included proclamations, starting with the first lines of that text, that were much more than mere rhetoric:

> Mankind is not essentially distinguished by the tongues spoken, the clothes worn, the lands occupied, or the dignities with which it is invested. The world is nothing but a huge republic, of which every nation is a family, and every individual a child. Our Society was at the outset established to revive and spread these essential maxims borrowed from the nature of man. We desire to reunite all men of enlightened mind, gentle manners, and agreeable wit, not only by a love for the fine arts, but much more by the grand principles of virtue, science, and religion, where the interests of the Fraternity shall become those of the whole human race, whence all nations shall be enabled to draw useful knowledge and where the subjects of all kingdoms shall learn to cherish one another without renouncing their own country.

In 1736, such statements were clearly not politically neutral.

Despite its formal secrets, exposed long ago, Masonry is not as discreet as it claims, and although it professes to be closed, it is in fact at least half open. Over time, it has therefore needed to cultivate a certain kind of relationship with society. Once again, different choices were made on either side of the Channel.

I. FREEMASONRY AND THE ESTABLISHMENT

In Great Britain, Freemasonry was formed at a time of religious peace, around a now uncontested political regime: the parliamentary monarchy. Pluralism and mutual tolerance were the watchwords. Since Freemasonry practiced these two principles in its Lodges, it is easy to see why, presumably, there could be no conflict with the authorities. This influenced the fate of the Grand Lodge: it became a part of the establishment.

In England, as in most countries that follow its example and share its culture, Masonry is a circle of social recognition. Its internal, ritual, and symbolic life is not particularly secret, and its public demonstrations are not rare, for example taking the form of solemn processions. It takes its leaders from the aristocracy and those holding high positions in the state or in society in general. Not so long ago, a newly initiated English Mason would inform his friends in the press, and could even invite them to a party to celebrate the event.

In such a religiously conformist and politically "neutral" view of Masonry, the proclaimed objective is to help mold citizens of a higher morality. The preferred expression of American Freemasons to describe the aim of Masonry is short and sweet: "to make good men better men." The only "externalization" that is accepted (and even strongly encouraged) is that of charitable work. Anglo-Saxon Grand Lodges devote huge sums of money to this each year, supporting numerous medical, research, and social aid institutions. In the United States in particular, these contributions are highly visible, and many hospitals even display the compass and the square, indicating the Masonic source of the funds donated to their work.

Yet this professed "apoliticism" is not as neutral as it appears. Is this social conformism not a subtle form of political conservatism? Significantly, in England, anti-Masonry (the prerogative of the Far Right in France) is highly left wing. Moreover, the situation has not always been this way: at the end of the eighteenth century in America, Freemasonry (not only via individual Brothers, but also sometimes through the involvement of whole Lodges) played an important part in triggering the revolution that brought independence.

Nevertheless, the Anglo-Saxon precedent created a first norm: Freemasonry does not criticize religions or get involved in social issues, and aims only to provide the community with good citizens. Even in France, many Masons still believe this today. Despite this, it is in France that another view emerged.

II. "SOCIETAL" FREEMASONRY

It is no exaggeration to say that in France at the end of the nineteenth century, Freemasonry had become an almost unanimously political organization. Nevertheless, it took almost two centuries for this situation to become established, as stated above.

Although the situation did take a new turn in the second half of the twentieth century (particularly because of the terrible persecution suffered during the Second World War), the political "temptation" of Freemasonry has remained a central element of this institution in France. Newspapers and magazines have regularly reported on it, attempting to establish the number of ministers, parliamentarians, and high-ranking officials who were Freemasons. The declarations of dignitaries, particularly from the Grand Orient de France, but also from several other Obediences who basically shared its sensibility, confirm this: a certain form of Freemasonry has clearly thought it should influence society and political life.

Nevertheless, even in its most "engaged" form, Masonry rarely demands political action as such: Lodges prefer to discuss "societal issues," undoubtedly because of the poor image of politicians and political parties over recent years. However, the boundary between "societal" recommendations and political positions is often unclear and permeable, particularly when the dignitaries speaking are themselves more or less official representatives or, in any case, active members of well-identified political parties: traditionally the Radical Party, but more often today, the Socialist Party.

This involvement of Masonry in politics is also, in the Masonic environment itself, a divisive issue: some openly reject it as nothing to do with Freemasonry, against its principles, and dangerous for its identity.

Divided on this issue, as on many others, French Masonry has therefore imagined various different doses of politics, symbolism, ritual, or spirituality in order to formulate its project.

In conclusion to this work, we will examine this Masonic project as a whole.

CHAPTER XIII
THE MASONIC PROJECT

In the above chapters, we have seen the complexity of Masonic procedure, which cannot be simplified to the various caricatures that are so popular. So what is the fundamental nature of the Masonic project, and what is its essential objective?

It is impossible to give an unequivocal answer to this question, but it is possible to identify at least three components that collectively allow every initiate to at least engage in a Masonic project: his own.

I. MASONIC HUMANISM

At the end of the 1980s, a then renowned Masonic writer, Paul Naudon, brought out a work entitled *L'Humanisme maçonnique. Essai sur l'existentialisme initiatique* (*Masonic Humanism: An Essay on Initiatory Existentialism*). With great conviction and talent, he defended the idea that by bringing together the intuitions of the Renaissance, the eighteenth-century Enlightenment thinkers, and the challenges of the disenchanted world announced by Max Weber, Freemasonry could offer a new path, between disappointing political engagements and religious positions that were now untenable.

We should note that the word *humanism*, with all its semantic ambiguity, and perhaps because of it, seems to be the best summary of how French Freemasons see Freemasonry. Beyond the contradictions that it can contain (and which it sometimes hides badly), it unites everyone around at least two ideas:

- The first is the deep attachment to human dignity, in its fullest form. Masonic humanism proclaims a message of hope in man's paradoxical ability to improve his nature through his own means. This is a positive and confident vision of man;

- The second central concept of Masonic humanism seems to be the respect for that essential dignity in every man, which means we must show him fraternal tolerance, and moral and material solidarity. From this perspective, the aim of human action is to allow all men to help their fellow men reach the full extent of their humanity. Again, this ambition can be achieved in various ways: some prefer discreet and individual "capillary" action in the here and now—"Freemasons everywhere, Freemasonry nowhere," as is sometimes said with a smile in Masonic circles. This is why, for example, there are many Freemasons in all associative networks; others prefer collective and public action, with a bigger role given to the open proclamations and demands of Freemasonry or one of its components (generally the different Obediences). "Freemasons everywhere, Freemasonry somewhere," as one Grand Master eloquently put it.

II. MASONIC ESOTERICISM

The esoteric dimension of Freemasonry, seemingly implied by its sometimes exotic symbolism and deliberately confusing rituals (not to mention the common hints of Kabbalism and Hermeticism), appears to impose on external perspectives. However, seen "from within" (the very meaning of *esôterikos*), this is not so apparent to all Freemasons. Some even explicitly claim an "esoteric Freemasonry," which implies that not all Freemasonry is esoteric.

Yet this break is not necessarily situated where we might expect. For example, English Masonry, strongly attached to a traditional theism, uses almost no esoteric speculation: it sees Masonic symbolism as a codified and unequivocal language which expresses age-old moral truths "veiled in allegory." However, in the diametrically opposed environment of secular Freemasonry, so heavily present in France, there is just as much distrust of esotericism, which is seen as a possible source of irrationalism and the feared religious dogmatism that follows.

We will not attempt to redefine esotericism here, but only to briefly evoke its status in the Masonic approach. Here, it is useful to refer to Antoine Faivre's two major studies (cited above), and to remember that esotericism is neither a set of doctrines nor an intrinsic quality of objects that can be described as esoteric. It is in fact a certain perspective on the world: a living world, filled with connections that trigger the creative imagination and suggest the experience of transformation. It cannot be denied that the Masonic "system," whatever the sensibility of the person who discovers or joins it, always includes this esoteric dimension to some degree.

From a psychological and moral perspective, some people see it as a way of establishing a purely human action, as it seems political declarations are now unable to do. Others see within it the possibility of a different perspective on themselves and the universe, allowing them to attempt to resolve the eternal enigmas of the human condition, to which it seems the traditional religions can no longer provide a satisfactory answer in a disenchanted world. Both groups nevertheless agree on a common method, which they strive to apply with sincerity, at the risk (which is actually an opportunity) of sharing their apparently different views with fraternity and mutual respect.

III. THE PATH OF INITIATION

In Masonic discourses, this is the ultimate expression that often encapsulates all that they want to say, and struggle to express clearly, about their engagement in Freemasonry: the "path of initiation." It is worth analyzing briefly.

The word "path" expresses the idea of a journey or process. Freemasonry is a search, a doubt greater than an initial uncertainty, a long series of questions, and the firm intention of always moving forwards, pushing on towards the discovery of the human, intellectual, moral, and spiritual unknown. It is much more hermeneutic than it is Hermetic. The journey is a great one, because nobody knows where it leads.

The word *initiation* primarily expresses the idea that everything must always be begun again (*initiare*: to begin), that nothing is ever definitively won, that men can never be certain, but that they must not become skeptical or discouraged. This doubt is even liberating, because it is the only thing that allows man to discover his true nature.

The path of initiation: this is how Freemasons refer to this unlikely cocktail, with its infinitely variable mixture between civic engagement and spiritual process that Freemasonry makes possible, indiscriminately, concurrently, or successively.

This is a path that they have been following for almost three centuries, sometimes courageously, sometimes without really believing in it. A single quality is required to join them: being a man or woman of good will . . .

BIBLIOGRAPHY

Bauer, Alain, and Roger Dachez. *Les 100 Mots de la franc-maçonnerie.* Paris: Puf, 2007.

Bauer, Alain, and Roger Dachez. *Les Rites maçonniques anglo-saxons.* Paris: Puf, 2010.

Bauer, Alain, and Gérard Meyer. *Le Rite français.* Paris: Puf, 2012.

Bauer, Alain, and Pierre Mollier. *Le Grand Orient de France.* Paris: Puf, 2012.

Dachez, Roger. *Histoire de la franc-maçonnerie française.* Paris: Puf, 2003.

Dachez, Roger. *Les Rites maçonniques égyptiens.* Paris: Puf, 2012.

Dachez, Roger and Jean-Marc Pétillot. *Le Rite écossais rectifié.* Paris: Puf, 2011.

Graesel, Alain. *La Grande Loge de France.* Paris: Puf, 2008.

Ligou, Daniel, ed. *Dictionnaire de la franc-maçonnerie.* Paris: Puf, 2006.

Murat, Jean. *La Grande Loge nationale française.* Paris: Puf, 2006.

Picart, Marie-France. *La Grande Loge féminine de France.* Paris: Puf, 2009.

Prat, Andrée. *L'Ordre maçonnique. Le droit humain.* Paris: Puf, 2003.

Saunier, Eric, ed. *Encyclopédie de la franc-maçonnerie.* Paris: Librairie générale française, 2000.

Viton, Yves-Max. *Le Rite écossais ancien et accepté.* Paris: Puf, 2012.

www.ingramcontent.com/pod-product-compliance
Lightning Source LLC
Chambersburg PA
CBHW021623270326
41931CB00008B/841